MUHAMMAD
AND
CHRIST

MUḤAMMAD
AND
CHRIST

Maulana Muḥammad 'Ali

MUHAMMAD
AND
CHRIST

Maulana Muhammad 'Ali

AUTHOR OF

English Translation of the Holy Qur'ān with Commentary (with Arabic text), *The Religion of Islam, Muhammad the Prophet, Early Caliphate, Living Thoughts of the Prophet Muhammad, A Manual of Hadith*; *Bayan al-Qur'ān* - Urdu translation and commentary of the Qur'ān in three volumes, *Fadl al-Bari* Translation and Commentary of *al-Sahih al-Bukharī* (Urdu), etc.

Published in U.S.A. by

Ahmadiyya Anjuman Ishā'at Islām Lahore Inc. (U.S.A.)
1315 Kingsgate Road, Columbus, Ohio 43221 U.S.A.

1993

First Published 1921

This Edition, re-typeset 1993

Copyright © 1993

Ahmadiyya Anjuman Ishā'at Islām Lahore Inc. (U.S.A.)
1315 Kingsgate Road, Columbus, Ohio 43221 U.S.A.

The Ahmadiyya Anjuman Ishā'at Islām *(Ahmadiyya Society for the propagation of Islām)*, is an international Muslim body devoted to the presentation of Islām through literary and missionary work. Since its inception in 1914, it has produced a range of highly acclaimed, standard books on all aspects of Islām, and has run Muslim missions in many parts of the world, establishing the first ever Islāmic centres in England (at Woking) and Germany (Berlin). The literature produced by the Anjuman, largely written by Maulana Muhammad Ali, is deep research work of the highest quality, based purely on the original sources of Islām. It has corrected many wrong notions about the religion of Islām, and has received world wide acclaim for its authenticity, scholarship and service of the faith.

Continuing the mission of *Haḍrat* Mirza Ghulām Aḥmad, the mujaddid of the 14th century Hijra and Promised Messiah, the Ahmadiyya Anjuman seeks to revive the original liberal, tolerant and rational spirit of Islām. It presents Islām as a great spiritual force for bringing about the moral reform of mankind, and shows that this religion has never advocated coercion, the use of physical force or the pursuit of political power in its support.

Information, books and free literature on Islām may be obtained by contacting *The Ahmadiyya Anjuman Ishā'at Islām Lahore* (or A.A.I.I.L.) at 1315 Kingsgate Road, Columbus, Ohio 43221 U.S.A.

Typesetting   Keywest Dataswitch Ltd.

Printers   Payette & Simms
                300 Arran Street
                St. Lambert, PQ
                Canada

Library of Congress card catalog number: **92-83853**
                                    ISBN: 0-913321-20-6

Contents

Transliteration

Below is explained the system of transliteration of proper names and Arabic words as adopted in this book. It follows the most recent rules recognized by European Orientalists with very slight variations.

’ stands for *hamza*, sounding like *h* in *hour*, a sort of catch in voice.

‘ stands for *‘ain*, sounding like a strong guttural *hamza*.

a sounds like *u* in *tub*.

ā sounds like *a* in *father*

ai sounds like *a* in *mat*; it represents a *fatha* before *yā*.

au sounds between *au* in *auto* and *o* in *more*; it represents a *fatha* before *wāo*.

d stands for *dāl*, being softer than *d*.

ḍ stands for *ḍād*, sounding between *d* and *z*.

gh stands for *ghain* (soft guttural *g*).

h sounds like *h* in *how*.

ḥ smooth guttural aspirate, sounds like *h* but is sharper.

i sounds as *i* in *pin*

ī sounds as *ee* in *deep*.

kh stands for *khā*, sounds like *ch* in the Scotch word *loch*.

q stands for *qaf*, strongly articulated guttural *k*.

ṣ stands for *sad*, strongly articulated, like *s* in *hiss*.

sh stands for *shīn*, sounding like *sh* in *she*.

t sounds like Italian dental, softer than *t*.

ṭ strongly articulated palatal *t*.

th sounds between *th* in *thing* and *s*.

u sounds like *u* in *pull*.

ū sounds like *oo* in *moot*.

ẓ strongly articulated palatal *z*.

Other letters sound as in English.

Introduction

One of the fundamental principles of Islām is a belief in all the prophets of the world, a belief in the fact that before the advent of the Holy Prophet Muḥammad, may peace and the blessings of God be upon him, different prophets had been raised among different nations. Thus the great change that the advent of the mighty Prophet of Arabia brought about was that the day of the national prophet was over to give place to the Great World Prophet, to the new order which was to bring about the unity of the whole human race. A belief in all the prophets of the world being thus the basic principle of the faith of Islām, the Muslims have always been averse to institute comparisons between the various prophets of the world, because comparisons, as they say, are odious. In fact, they were forbidden by the Prophet himself to do so unnecessarily lest in the heat of controversy on such points, things might be said which may be derogatory to the dignity of a prophet. At the same time the Holy Qur'ān declares in plain words that there are varying degrees of excellence even among the prophets:

> We have made some of these apostles to excel others.[1]

It must, however, be borne in mind that it is one thing to say that one prophet possesses an excellence which another does not, and quite another to speak of that other in derogatory words. The prophets were all perfect men raised for the regeneration of man, but they no doubt possessed varying degrees of excellence according to the nature of the work with which they were entrusted and the capabilities of the race for whose regeneration they were raised. It is in this light, therefore, that we take up the challenge so often given by the Christians as to the comparative greatness of Muḥammad or Christ, a task which, though painful, is necessary because of the wrong inferences drawn from the sacred Book of Islām.

---

1. 2:253

1

The error which Christian writers generally commit is that they place all reliance on words, not caring for the work actually done; they look to appearances, not reality. With them greatness consists in the terms of eulogy which may be heaped upon a person and the incredibly wonderful stories which may be narrated of him, not in the actual work done by him. Hence they are always contending that Jesus speaks of himself thus, not so Muhammad, peace be on him, or that the founder of Christianity performed so many miracles which the founder of Islām did not. The Holy Qur'ān, on the other hand, adopts a different attitude towards this question, regarding work, not words or miracles, as the criterion of greatness. It speaks of the greatness of the Holy Prophet not in the words of eulogy in which Jesus Christ speaks of himself according to the Gospels, but by drawing attention to the great change, the mighty transformation, that he brought about in the world. It does not speak, except in rare instances, even of his great miracles which are, however, recorded in collections of reports; in fact, it looks upon all miracles as matters of secondary importance in comparison with the greatest of all miracles, the miracle of planting virtue and supplanting evil in the world, the miracle of taking up men from the depth of degradation and raising them to the highest dignity which they are capable of rising to. And why are miracles wrought, after all? They do not serve any purpose in themselves; they are not the end but the means to the great end of the spiritual regeneration of the world. It is for this reason that the Holy Qur'ān does not speak of the Holy Prophet in high-sounding words, nor does it lay much stress on his miracles, but speaks again and again of the wonderful transformation which he wrought, a transformation so unique in the history of the world that the writer of the article on the *Koran* in the *Encyclopædia Britannica* (eleventh edition) speaks of him as the "most successful of all prophets and religious personalities," an admission which far outweighs all the high-sounding words and wonderful stories of the miracles narrated in the Gospels.

The Christian controversialist of to-day, however, seems to think that he has another way out of the difficulty. He bases the superiority of Christ to other prophets, not on the Gospels, but on the Holy

Qur'ān. A strange allegation indeed! The Qur'ān which, on the one hand, is denounced to be the fabrication of an impostor is brought forward, on the other, as the testimony supporting the extravagant claims advanced for Jesus Christ. The position of the Christian controversialist here is quite inexplicable, but we need not be surprised at it as matters far more important relating to the Christian religion are as inexplicable. It is said that the Holy Qur'ān speaks of Jesus Christ in words of high praise. Quite so; but at the same time it mentions him as only one among the numerous Israelite prophets who followed Moses; it describes him to be an apostle bearing a message limited to a single nation:

And an apostle to the children of Israel.[2]

This description is sufficient to show that the Holy Qur'ān cannot consistently place him in a position of superiority to the other prophets, to say nothing of the great World Prophet whose message is expressly stated to be for the whole human race. But what a Christian is unable to see is, why should the Qur'ān speak of a prophet of another nation in words of praise? In fact, he is unable to differentiate between the Gospels and the Holy Qur'ān in this respect. The message of Jesus was for the Israelites and therefore he had nothing to do with other prophets; the message of Muḥammad, may peace and the blessings of God be upon him, was for the whole world and therefore the Holy Qur'ān speaks of the prophets of the whole world. And as in addition it required a belief in all the prophets, therefore it was necessary for it to preach respect for all of them. Now at the time of its advent Jesus Christ and his mother were two of the sacred personages whose names were held in the greatest abhorrence by the Israelites, to which nation they belonged. Mary was falsely accused of adultery, and her son was denounced as the offspring of illicit intercourse and as a liar. The Holy Qur'ān had to sweep away these calumnies to establish the great principle of the righteousness of all prophets. Those who lay much stress on the words of praise for Jesus Christ and his mother in the Holy Qur'ān

---

2. 3:48

must remember that the false allegations of the Jews against these two righteous persons required a mention of their virtues and their greatness, and the very fact that other prophets were not denounced in such evil terms made a mention of their virtues unnecessary.

If, however, it is inconsistent in a Christian to base the alleged superiority of Jesus Christ to the Holy Prophet on a book which he condemns as the work of an impostor, it is stranger still that wild statements are often made in making out a case for Jesus which are not only opposed to the Holy Qur'ān, but which even the Gospels, the sacred scriptures of the Christian religion, condemn to be false and conclusions are drawn from the words of the Holy Qur'ān which are not only quite foreign to its intent but which are also belied by the Gospels. In dealing with this question therefore I shall have to refer both to the Holy Qur'ān and the Bible, especially the Gospels. But as regards the reliability which can be placed upon the material drawn from these two sources, there is a world of difference and the circumstances under which the Gospels were written and transmitted make it necessary to accept their statements very guardedly.

As regards the authenticity of the Holy Qur'ān, I need not detain the reader very long. From one end of the world to the other, from China in the Far East to Morocco and Algeria in the Far West, from the scattered islands of the Pacific Ocean to the great desert of Africa, the Qur'ān is one, and no copy differing in even a diacritical point is met with in the possession of one among the four hundred millions of Muslims. There are, and always have been, contending sects, but the same Qur'ān is in the possession of one and all. Political dissensions and doctrinal differences grew up within a quarter of a century after the death of the Holy Prophet, but no one ever raised a voice against the purity of the text of the Holy Qur'ān. A manuscript with the slightest variation in the text is unknown. Even Dr. Mingana has been unable to show any but mistakes due to carelessness in copying or transcription by inexperienced hands in his "Leaves from three ancient Qur'āns". And the original manuscript copies made and circulated under the orders of the third successor of the Holy Prophet have been safely preserved to this day. Here is the opinion of a hostile critic:

The recension of Othman has been handed down to us unaltered ... contending and embittered factions taking their rise in the murder of Othman himself within a quarter of a century from the death of Mohamet, have ever since rent the Mohametan world. Yet but One Coran has been current amongst them; and the consentaneous use by all of the same scripture in every age to the present day is an irrefragable proof that we have now before us the very text prepared by command of the unfortunate Caliph. *There is probably in the world no other work which has remained twelve centuries with so pure a text*

(Muir's *Life of Mohamet*; italics are mine).

The same author goes on to show that the copy made by 'Uthmān was a faithful reproduction of the copy made by Zaid only six months after the death of the Holy Prophet and that Zaid's edition was a faithful copy of the revelations of the Holy Prophet, giving a number of reasons for believing so, and the conclusion to which he comes is that he agrees with the verdict of Von Hammer: "That we hold *the Coran to be as surely Mohamet's word as the Mohametans hold it to be the word of God.*"

The story of the authorship and transmission of the Gospels is, however, quite different. The earliest existing manuscript that was found in 1859 is a Greek manuscript which, we are told, was made about the middle of the fourth century after Jesus Christ. Being found on Mount Sinai in the Convent of St. Catherine it is known as the Siniaticus. Another known as the Alexandrinus which is now in the British Museum belongs to the fifth century. Another called the Vatican belongs to the fourth century but is incomplete. And these are said to be the three chief manuscripts. As to their condition and reliability I will quote, not a critic, but a commentator of the Bible, the Rev. J.R. Dummelow:

> To begin with, the writers of the Gospels report in Greek (although they may have had some Aramaic sources) the sayings of Jesus Christ who for the most part probably spoke Aramaic. Nor is it likely that these writers or their copyists

had any idea that their record would go beyond the early Churches with which they themselves were familiar.

The same applies to St. Paul. His letters, now so valued, were messages only intended for the Churches to which they were addressed. Those who first copied them would not regard them at all "sacred" in our sense of the word.

Nor even in the later centuries do we find that scrupulous regard for the sacred text which marked the transmission of the Old Testament. A copyist would sometimes put in not what was in the text, but what he thought ought to be in it. He would trust a fickle memory, or he would even make the text accord with the views of the school to which he belonged. Besides this, an enormous number of copies are preserved. In addition to the versions and quotations from the early Christian Fathers, nearly four thousand Greek manuscripts of the New Testament are known to exist. As a result, the variety of readings is considerable.

What reliance can be placed on documents which were transmitted so carelessly and with such additions and alterations by the scribes? Even their authorship and the date of writing is absolutely uncertain. The first of the canonical Gospels is advertised as the Gospel according to St. Matthew, who was an Apostle. But it is certain that that Gospel was never written by him. It was written by some unknown hand. The story of its authorship as given by the commentator, whom I have quoted above, is that probably St. Matthew had written in Hebrew a book of "logia" or "oracles," which is not to be met with anywhere, except that Papias writing in A.D. 130 credits St. Matthew with the composition of such a book.

> Of a Greek translation of these "Logia" our author seems to have made such liberal use, that he acknowledged his obligations to the Apostle by calling his work "according to Matthew."

This explanation speaks for itself. St. Matthew may have written a certain book which is not met with anywhere except in the reference in Papias. The rest is all a conjecture. There is not the least evidence that the unknown author of the first Gospel had a copy of this book or of its translation in Greek, nor that he made any liberal use of it. The conjecture is based simply on the fact that he called it the Gospel according to St. Matthew, but he might have done it as well if he had only the oral traditions of St. Matthew.

The next Gospel is that of St. Mark, who was a companion of St. Peter, and the following testimony as recorded by Papias about A.D. 130 is relied upon in ascribing the authorship of the Gospel to him:

> Mark having become (or having been) Peter's interpreter wrote all that he remembered (or, all that Peter related) though he did not (record) in order that which was said or done by Christ. For he neither heard the Lord nor followed Him; but subsequently, as I said, (attached himself) to Peter who used to frame his teaching to meet the (immediate) wants (of his hearers); and not as making a connected narrative of the Lord's discourses.

Even if we accept this evidence, the Gospel of St. Mark may be said to have been based on the oral tradition of Peter, but even this evidence does not make it certain that the Gospel in our hands was actually written by St. Mark and higher criticism favours the view that he was only the author of the nucleus of the present Gospel ascribed to him.

St. Luke too was not a disciple of Jesus but a disciple of the Apostles and he is said to have followed St. Paul. And as regards the fourth Gospel, there is no doubt that it is a much later composition. As regards the dates of the various Gospels, the most favourable view as regards the first three Gospels is that they were written about the year A.D. 70, but higher criticism favours a much later date, and internal evidence is regarded to point to this conclusion. In a discussion as to the date of canonical Matthew we are told that "many are disposed to bring down the date of the entire Gospel as late as to A.D. 130." An earlier date can only be admitted if a great many passages are treated as later interpolations. As regards the date of St. Luke the conclusion arrived at is that "the year A.D. 100 will be the superior, and somewhere about A.D. 110 the inferior, limit of the date of its composition"[3].

The considerations as to the authorship, the date and transmission of the Gospels, the very large variety of manuscripts and readings and the undeniable existence of interpolations in them reduce their credibility to the minimum; and hence a critisicm of them in the *Encyclopædia Biblica* leads the Rev. E.A. Abbot to raise a very important question:

> The forgoing sections may have sometimes seemed to raise a doubt whether any credible elements were to be found in the Gospels at all.

The answer to this question is that in all the Gospels, the following five passages may be treated as surely credible:

(1) The passage that shows that Jesus refused to be called sinless: "Why callest thou me good? There is none good but one, that is, God".[4]

(2) The passage that shows that he held that blasphemy against himself could be forgiven: "All manner of sin and blasphemy shall be forgiven unto men: but the blasphemy against the Holy Ghost shall not be forgiven unto men".[5]

(3) The passage that shows that his own mother and brethren had no faith in him and they sincerely thought that he was mad: And when his friends heard of it, they went out to lay hold on him; for they said, He is beside himself'.[6] From v. 31 it appears that these friends were his own mother and his brothers.

(4) The passage that shows that Jesus Christ had no knowledge of the unseen: "Of that day and of that hour knoweth no one, not even the angels in heaven, neither the son but the Father."

(5) The passage that speaks of the cry of despair that he uttered on the cross: "My God, My God, why hast Thou forsaken me".[7]

---

3. *Encyclopædia Biblica*   4. Mark 10:18   5. Mark 12:31
6. Mark 3:21   7. Matt. 27:44

To these five are added four others dealing with his miracles which will be referred to in the discussion on his miracles later on, and these nine passages are said to be "the foundation-pillar for a truly scientific life of Jesus."

It would thus be seen that the basis of the Christian religion is laid on the most unreliable record, and the stories of the miracles wrought and the wonderful deeds done, on which is based the doctrine of the Divinity of Jesus Christ and of his superiority to all mortals, can therefore be only received with the greatest caution. It must, however, be borne in mind that mere superiority of Jesus Christ as a mortal to another mortal, says the Holy Founder of Islām, does not bring us a whit nearer the truth of the Christian religion unless it is shown that he possessed a Divine nature or that he did deeds which no mortal has ever done. If the Christian religion had followed the principles laid down by the earlier prophets, the assertion that Jesus Christ was a greater man than any other human being that ever lived, would have done some good to the cause of Christianity, but so long as the atonement of the sins of men by a Divine person remains the central doctrine of that religion, nothing less than a clear proof that his superiority to other mortals lay in being Divine and above a mortal can be of any use to its cause. It is in this light that a discussion of the relative merits of Christianity and Islām, or of the relative greatness of their founders, can really help a seeker after truth. But as Christian controversy finds itself unable to cope with this question, I will take the various points as they are raised by Christian controversialists. I take the Christian case as presented in the latest of their pamphlets, a small tract issued by the Christian Missionary Society at Ludhiana, under the title of *Haqā'iq-i Qur'ān*, or the "Qurānic Truths" which claims to have been based only on "the Qurānic statements," and which has been circulated and broadcast in India and, through the pages of *Muslim World*, in all Christian and Muslim countries.

Chapter 1
Miracles

1. General Remarks

The Gospels are full of the stories of the miracles wrought by Jesus Christ and in them, as in nothing else, is thought to lie the argument of his Divinity. Even the central fact in the Christian religion is a miracle: if Jesus did not rise from among the dead the Christian faith and the preaching of Christianity is in vain. Religious duties, normal teachings and spiritual awakening do not occupy the place which miracles do in the Gospels. The dead are made to rise from their graves, multitudes of the sick are healed, water is turned into wine, devils are cast out, and many other wonderful deeds are done. Suppose for the sake of argument that this record of Gospels is literally true; what was the effect of this on the lives of those who witnessed these miracles? The miraculous in a prophet's life is needed to assure the people of the truth of his message and to convince the ordinary mind that being a possessor of extraordinary powers he must be followed in spiritual matters. The bringing about of a moral and spiritual transformation is admittedly the real object, the miraculous being only needed as a help towards the attainment of that object. The former at most may be looked upon as the means to an end, the latter is the end itself. The best evidence of miracles thus consists in the effect they produce.

The most important question for us therefore is: supposing Jesus wrought all the miracles recorded in the Gospels, what was the result? How great was the success he attained in bringing about a transformation? One Gospel tells us that Jesus was followed by multitudes of sick persons who were all healed, another says that many were healed. Now, if either of these statements were true, not a single person should have been left in the land who should not have believed in Jesus. It is inconceivable that those who saw such extraordinary deeds done by Jesus Christ should have rejected him as a liar. They saw the sick healed and the dead raised to life and yet they all disbelieved in him as if not a single miracle had been wrought! And how strange that even the great multitudes that were healed do not seem to have been believers in Jesus, though the Gospels tell us that faith was a condition prior to being healed; for if even these multitudes had believed in Jesus he would have had a following at the time of his crucifixion far more numerous than he actually had, and sufficiently large to baffle the authorities.

But what do we find? The following of Jesus is poor, not only as regards number, but also as regards its character. From among the five hundred that followed him he chose twelve who were to sit on twelve thrones, who were to be entrusted with the work after the Master, and these twelve showed a strange weakness of character, the greatest of them, Peter, denying Jesus thrice for fear of being treated harshly by the enemies, and not even hesitating to curse when he thought that a curse was the only means of escape. The others even durst not approach Jesus, while one of the chosen ones turned out to be a traitor. On an earlier occasion when Jesus asked them to pray for him, he found them all asleep. Often had he to rebuke them for having no faith. Who was it in the world on whom the miraculous deeds of Jesus, if they were ever done, made an impression? The mere fact that Jesus was unable to bring about any transformation either on his friends or foes, is a sufficient testimony that the stories of miracles were invented afterwards.

The poorness of the result attained by Jesus Christ notwithstanding all the stories of miracles becomes the more prominent when compared with the wonderful results attained by the great World Prophet that appeared in Arabia. The Holy Prophet had before him a nation which had never before been guided to truth, among whom no prophet had appeared before him, the attempts at whose reformation by both the Jews and the Christians had proved an utter failure. This nation had, both as regards material civilisation and moral calibre, been sunk in the depth of degradation, and for centuries the voice of the reformers had fallen on deaf ears. Yet within less than a quarter of a century a wonderful transformation was brought about. The old evils had all disappeared, and ignorance and superstition had given place to love of knowledge and learning. From the disunited elements of a people who did not deserve the name of a nation had sprung up a living and united nation before whose onward march in the world the greatest nations of the world were powerless and whose civilisation and knowledge fed the world for long centuries. But this material advancement was only the result of an inner change, of a moral and spiritual transformation, the equal of which has not been witnessed in the world. Thus both morally and materially, Muḥammad, may peace and the blessings of God be upon him, raised a nation from the depths of degradation to the highest plane of advancement. As against this, what did Jesus do? He had before him the Jewish nation read in scriptures and practising many virtues at least externally. He also found them living under a civilised government with advantages of a material civilisation to help their progress. In spite of these advantages he was unable to produce the least change in the life of that nation as a whole. If the effect was so poor, it is impossible that anything great was done. In this light, the stories of the miracles are clearly pure inventions or exaggerations made to compensate for the apparent failure.

A critical examination of the Gospels leads to the same conclusion. Mark 8:12 contains a plain denial of signs:

> And he sighed deeply in his spirit, and saith, Why doth this generation seek after a sign? Verily I say unto you, There shall no sign be given unto this generation.

Similar statements are contained in the other Gospels; see Matt. 12:39; 16:4; Luke 11:29.

> Then certain of the Scribes and the Pharisees answered, saying, Master, we would see a sign from thee. But he answered and said unto them, An evil and adulterous

generation seeketh after a sign; and there shall no sign be given to it, but the sign of the prophet Jonas.[8]

Here we have a plain denial to show any sign except the one sign of Jonas, which is understood by some commentators as meaning the sign of preaching, by others as remaining in the grave (alive of course, as Jonas was) for three days and three nights. If Jesus worked such great wonders, how was it that the Pharisees asked for a sign and how was it that Jesus refused to show any sign. In answer to their demand, he ought to have referred to the testimony of the thousands that had been healed; in fact, the masses around him should have silenced the questioners by their evidence. But no such thing happened. The commentators say that the Pharisees asked for a greater sign than the healing of the sick "to which they were *accustomed*." If it was indeed so, then too it is clear that Jesus' healing of the sick was nothing extraordinary. And why did not Jesus refer to his raising of the dead?

Again, Mark tells us that Jesus was unable to do any mighty work in Nazareth, save healing a few sick persons: "And he could there do no mighty work, save that he laid his hands upon a few sick folk, and healed them." This too shows Jesus' inability to work any miracle, the healing of the sick being looked upon as a very ordinary occurrence. These statements are a clear evidence that the stories of wonderful works were invented afterwards, or at least there is much exaggeration in them.

2. Raising the Dead to Life

The mightiest work of Jesus is said to be the raising of the dead to life, and it is in this, we are told, that the proof of Christ's divinity is met with. Here is the argument:

Christ's raising the dead to life is admitted by the Muslims on the basis of the Holy Qur'ān, and raising the dead to life

---

8. Matt. 12:38, 39

is beyond the power of man and only an attribute of Divine Being ... And in this attribute of Divinity no other mortal partakes with Jesus.

As to what the Holy Qur'ān says, we shall see later on. Let us first closely consider the claim made on the basis of the Christian sacred scriptures. The argument is that Jesus is a Divine person because he raised the dead to life. This argument could only be advanced by a man who believed that no other mortal had ever raised the dead to life. But the Bible belies this argument. It contains instances of other mortals who raised the dead to life, and therefore even if Jesus actually wrought this miracle, the inference of his divinity from it is quite illogical; or if he was Divine because he raised the dead to life, Elisha had as much divinity in him. In 2 Kings 4 we are told that a child had died and his death had been well made sure when Elisha came in:

> And when Elisha was come into the house, behold, the child was dead, and laid upon his bed. He went in therefore, and shut the door upon them twain, and prayed unto the Lord ... and the child sneezed seven times, and the child opened his eyes.[9]

Elijah also raised the dead to life.

> And he cried unto the Lord, and said, O Lord, my God, hast thou also brought evil upon the widow with whom I sojourn, by slaying her son? ... I pray thee, let this child"s soul come into him again. And the Lord heard the voice of Elijah; and the soul of the child came into him again and he revived.[10]

Thus the Bible does not give to Jesus any exclusive claim to divinity on the score of raising the dead to life. Indeed, in one respect Elisha's power of raising the dead to life was greater than that of Jesus, for even his dry bones after his death had the efficacy of giving life to a dead man:

---

9. 2 Kings 4:32-35 10. 1 Kings 17:19-22

> And it came to pass as they were burying a man ... and they
> cast the man into the sepulchre of Elisha: and when the man
> was let down and touched the bones of Elisha, he revived
> and stood up on his feet.[11]

It is sometimes asserted that Jesus wrought the miracles by his own
power, while in the case of other prophets, it was God Who worked
the miracles through them. This fantastic distinction does not prove
of much value, for in the case of Jesus too it was God Who did the
miracles:

> Ye men of Israel, hear these words; Jesus of Nazareth, a man
> approved of God among you by miracles and wonders and
> signs, which God did by him in the midst of you.[12]

It is very probable that the stories of Elijah and Elisha raising the
dead to life produced the pious desire in the minds of the early
followers of Jesus Christ to ascribe similar deeds to their Master.
There are clear traces of this in the narratives themselves. Matthew,
Mark and Luke narrate the raising of the ruler's daughter about
whom Matthew quotes Jesus as saying: "The maid is not dead but
sleepeth."[13] The others omit these words, but their presence in
Matthew is sufficient to disclose the nature of this miracle. It is
remarkable that John does not speak of this miracle at all but
mentions instead a miracle which is not known to the Synoptists, *viz.*
the raising of Lazarus after he had been in the grave for four days.[14]
How did it happen that the Synoptists, one and all, had no knowledge
of such a great miracle, and how was it that John had no knowledge
of the raising of the ruler's daughter? The inference is clear that
John, writing later, had his doubts about the raising of the ruler's
daughter, and he instead made some symbolical story read as if it
were an actual occurrence. In addition to these two miracles, Luke
alone mentions a third case, the raising of the widow's son at Nain,[15]
which is known neither to the other Synoptists nor to John.

---

11. 2 Kings 13:21   12. Acts 2:22   13. 9:24   14. 11:38-44
15. 7:11-17

We may, however, refer here to the height of absurdity to which the love of wonderful stories carried the early Christian writers. Matthew was not satisfied with the single miracle of raising the sleeping girl, and he therefore makes the dead rise out of the graveyard and walk into Jerusalem as soon as Jesus gave up the ghost:

> And behold the veil of the temple was rent in twain from the top to the bottom; and the earth did quake, and the rocks rent; and the graves were opened; and many bodies of the saints which slept arose, and came out of the graves after his resurrection and went into the holy city and appeared unto many.[16]

This wonderful miracle passes all imagination: only the evangelist does not give the details as to what clothes these skeletons had on as they walked into the city; as in the case of Lazarus, the writer is careful enough to add that the dead man came forth bound hand and foot with grave clothes: and his face was bound about with a napkin and an order to loose him had to be given by Jesus Christ. Probably the grave clothes of these saints who had perhaps been dead for centuries, or at any rate for long years, had been preserved intact to assist in the performance of the miracle. Not all the commentators have the courage to read this wonderful story literally, and accordingly we have the following comment by the Rev. J.R. Dummelow:

> This incident seems to be a pictorial setting forth of the truth that in the Resurrection of Christ is involved the Resurrection of all his saints, so that on Easter Day all Christians may be said in a certain sense to have risen with him.

Herein lies the truth about all the miracles of raising the dead to life. Jesus talked in parables, and symbolical language was used by him freely. "'Let the dead bury their dead', said he".[17] And again:

---

16. 27:51-53   17. Matt. 8:22

Verily, verily, I say unto you, He that heareth my word and believeth in Him that sent me, hath everlasting life, and shall not come into condemnation, but is passed from death unto life. Verily, verily, I say unto you, The hour is coming, and now is, when the dead shall hear the voice of the son of God: and they that hear shall live ... Marvel not at this; for the hour is coming in which all that are in the graves shall hear His voice and shall come forth.

Now in all these cases, by the *dead*, even by *those in the graves*, are meant the spiritually dead, those dead in sin, and by life is meant the life spiritual. Similar figurative language was used by the Jews. According to a Jewish tradition, "the wicked, though living, are termed dead." Jesus Christ sent word to John the Baptist:

Go and show John again those things which ye do hear and see: The blind receive their sight, and the lame walk, the lepers are cleansed, and the deaf hear, the dead are raised up, and the poor have the gospel preached to them.[18]

The concluding words of this message throw light on what Jesus meant, for he was not actually preaching the Gospel to only *the poor*. He was talking symbolically, but his words being misunderstood, it was thought necessary to add to the story of his life these stories of the raising of the dead to life. The whole fault lies in Jesus' too free use of the symbolic language so that it was not the Jews alone who had to be told that they did not understand his symbolic language,[19] but even the disciples often misunderstood him, taking his symbolic language in a literal sense. The following incident is worth noting:

Now the disciples had forgotten to take bread ... And he charged them, saying, Take heed, beware of the leaven of the Pharisees, and of the leaven of Herod. And they reasoned among themselves, saying, It is because we have no bread. And when Jesus knew it, he saith unto them, Why reason ye, because ye have no bread? Perceived ye not yet, neither

---

18. Matt. 11:4, 5   19. John 8:43

understand? Have ye your heart hardened? Having eyes see
ye not?[20]

Indeed we find the disciples themselves complaining of his
resorting too much to symbolic language and pleading their inability
to follow him. Herein lies the solution of the stories of raising the
dead to life.

Next we come to what the Holy Qur'ān says about the raising of
the dead to life. To say that the Holy Qur'ān speaks of Jesus
exclusively as raising the dead to life betrays sheer ignorance of its
contents. It speaks as clearly of the Holy Prophet raising the dead to
life. Thus it says:

> O you who believe, answer the call of Allāh and His Apostle
> when he calls you to that which gives you life!.[21]

The mistake arises from the invidious distinction made between the
prophets of God, so that when the Holy Qur'ān speaks of the Holy
Prophet raising the dead to life, the meaning is said to be the giving
of spiritual life to those who were dead in ignorance, but when it
speaks of Jesus' raising the dead to life, the words are looked upon
as meaning the bringing back to life of those who were dead
physically. Why should not the same meaning be attached to the
same words in both places? As to what that meaning is, the Holy
Qur'ān explains itself. It speaks of the dead again and again and
means the spiritually dead. It speaks of raising them to life and
means the life spiritual. I will give a few examples to show this, as
this point has been much misunderstood. It says in one place:

> Is he who was dead, then We raised him to life and made for
> him a light by which he walks among the people, like him
> whose likeness is that of one in utter darkness whence he
> cannot come forth?"[22]

Here we have the *dead man raised to life* in clear words, yet by this
description is meant not one whose soul has departed from, and been

---

20. Mark 8:14-17   21. 8:24   22. 6:123

brought back to, this body of clay, but one whose death and life are both spiritual. In another place we have:

> Surely you do not make the dead to hear, nor make the deaf to hear, when they go back retreating.[23]

Mark the combination here of the *dead* with the *deaf*. They are both placed in the same category. The Prophet cannot make them *hear* when they do not stay to listen and go back *retreating*. In the same sense it is stated elsewhere:

> Neither are the living and the dead alike. Surely Allāh makes whom He pleases hear, and you cannot make those hear who are in the graves.[24]

Here it is not only the *dead*, but those who are *in the graves*. Yet the dead bodies that rest in their coffins beneath the earth are not meant. Nor are the words to be taken as meaning that the Prophet cannot give life to those who are spiritually in the graves. What is implied is only this that the Prophet as a mere mortal could not do what was almost impossible, the giving of life to those who were in their graves: it was the hand of Allāh working in the Prophet that would bring about such a mighty change.

It is clear from this that when the Holy Qur'ān speaks of the prophets of God as raising the dead to life, it is spiritual death and spiritual life to which it refers, and it is in this sense that it speaks of the Holy Prophet Muḥammad and Jesus Christ as raising the dead to life. This becomes the more clear when it is considered that according to the Holy Qur'ān the dead shall actually be raised to life only on the day of Judgement and their *return to this life* before the Great Day is prohibited in the clearest words. Thus:

> Allāh takes the souls at the time of their death, and those that die not, during their sleep; then He withholds those on whom He has passed the decree of death and sends the others back till an appointed time.[25]

---

23. 27:80   24. 35:22   25. 39:42

This verse affords a conclusive proof that the Holy Qur'ān does not admit the return to life in this world of those who are actually dead. Once the decree of death is passed, the soul is withheld and under no circumstances is it sent back. The same principle is affirmed in the following verses:

> Until when death overtakes one of them, he says: Send me back, my Lord, send me back, haply I may do good in that which I have left. By no means! it is a mere word that he speaks, and against them is a barrier until the day they are raised.[26]

Thus we are told in the clearest possible words that no one who has passed through the door of death into the state of *barzakh* is allowed to go back into the previous state.

A third verse may also be quoted:

> And it is binding on a town which We destroy that they shall not return.[27]

A few words of comment may be added to this last verse from a saying of the Holy Prophet. The following incident is recorded in *Nisā'ī* and *Ibn Mājah*, two out of the six authentic collections of reports. Jābir's father 'Abdullāh was slain in a battle with the enemies of Islam. The Holy Prophet one day saw Jābir dejected. "What makes you dejected?" asked the affectionate Teacher of his sorrowful companion. "My father died and he has left behind a large family and a heavy debt" was the reply. "May I not give you the good news of the great favour that your father met with from Allāh?" said the Holy Prophet ... "God said, O My servant! express a wish and I will grant you. He said, My Lord! give me life so that I may fight in Thy cause again and be slain once more. The word has gone forth from Me, said the Mighty Lord, that they shall not return." The pious wish of 'Abdullāh to come back to life and fight the enemies of Islām had only one barrier in its way — "that they shall not return," — these words being exactly the concluding words of the

---

26. 23:99, 100   27. 21:95

verse I have quoted last. Similar evidence as to the Holy Prophet's comment on this verse is met with in the *Sahih Muslim*, where the martyrs are generally spoken of in almost the same words. "What more do you desire?" they are asked by the Almighty. "What more may we wish for, our Lord?" is the reply. The question is repeated and they say: "Our Lord, we desire that Thou shouldst send us back to the world that we may fight again in Thy cause." And what is the reply to this holy wish at a time when the addition of a single person to the ranks of Islām was looked upon as the greatest Divine favour? "I have written *that they shall not return*." Nothing in the world can subvert the clear dictum of the Holy Qur'ān that those once dead shall not return to life in this world; and the return to life shall only take place on the great day of Resurrection.

3. Healing the Sick

Although Jesus' miracles of healing do not occupy a very high place in the record of miracles, not even among the great and wonderful deeds which man may do, yet it is probable that most of these stories had their origin in figurative speech or in exaggeration. Here too Elijah and Elisha stand on the same footing with him. Elisha healed Naaman of leprosy,[28] and restored eyes to a whole people who were first made blind miraculously:

> And when they came down to him Elisha prayed unto the Lord, and said, Smite this people, I pray thee, with blindness. And he smote them with blindness according to the word of Elisha ... And it came to pass, when they were come into Samaria, that Elisha said, Lord, open the eyes of these men, that they may see. And the Lord opened their eyes, and they saw.[29]

---

28. 2 Kings 5:1-14 29. 2 Kings 6:17-20

For some other mighty works done by the Old Testament prophets, see 2 Kings 4:1-7, 14-17, 40, 44; 2:8, 14, 19-22; 6:5-6; Joshua 3:17; Ezk. 37:10, etc.

If these great miracles of healing the sick had been limited to the prophets, as they are in the Old Testament, they would have retained at least the halo of dignity about them. But when we come to the New Testament period, the miracles of healing become a very common thing. When accused by the Pharisees that he cast out devils with the help of Beelzebub, Jesus answered, "And if I by Beelzebub cast out devils, by whom do your children cast them out".[30] Here therefore is a plain admission put into the mouth of Jesus that even the disciples of the Pharisees who were opposed to Jesus Christ could work miracles of healing, or of casting out the devils, as the writers of the Gospels would have it. Again we are told that a man who did not follow Jesus was working the same miracles as Jesus in those very days:

> Master, we saw one casting out devils in thy name, and he followeth not us ... But Jesus said, Forbid him not; for there is no man which shall do a miracle in my name that can lightly speak evil of me.[31]

And similarly those whom Jesus rejects in the final judgement as worders of iniquity did wonderful works:

> Many will say to me in that day, Lord, Lord, have we not prophesied in thy name? and in thy name have cast out devils? and in thy name done many wonderful works?[32]

Nay, even false prophets could show great signs: "For there shall arise false Christs, and false prophets, and shall show great signs and wonders."[33]

The strangest of all is the story of the healing pool which St. John records in his Gospel:

---

30. Matt. 12:27, Luke 11:19   31. Mark 9:38, 39   32. Matt. 7:22
33. Matt. 24:24

Now there is at Jerusalem by the sheep-market a pool, which is called in the Hebrew tongue Bethesda, having five porches. In these lay a great multitude of impotent folk, of blind, halt, withered, waiting for the moving of the water. For an angel went down at a certain season into the pool, and troubled the water: whosoever then first after the troubling of the water stepped in was made whole of whatsoever disease he had.[34]

The revised version omits the latter portion as an interpolation but even then the difficulty of the healing-pool having the same power as the "son of God" is not surmounted.

These little anecdotes recorded by the Gospels take the whole force out of the argument of miracles. Any Christian who has read the Gospels dare not speak of these miracles as evidence of even the truth of Christ as a prophet, to say nothing of his divinity. But what is worse, the Gospel statements show clear signs of exaggeration, and one evangelist has tried to enrich the dry details of another. I would not here go into details, but would instead refer the reader to the conclusion arrived at by a Christian critic in the *Encyclopædia Biblica*:

> The conclusion is inevitable that even the one evangelist whose story in any particular case involves less of the supernatural than that of the others, is still very far from being entitled on that account to claim implicit acceptance of his narrative. Just in the same degree in which those who come after him have gone beyond him, it is easily conceivable that he himself may have gone beyond those who went before him.

And again:

> It is not at all difficult to understand how the contemporaries of Jesus, after seeing some wonderful deed or deeds wrought by him which they regarded as miracles, should have

---

34. John 5:2-4

credited him with every other kind of miraculous power without distinguishing, as the modern mind does, between those miracles which are amenable to physical influences and those which are not. It is also necessary to bear in mind that the cure may after all have been only temporary.[35]

In addition to the influence of exaggeration on the stories of the marvellous, there was the mistaking of the spiritual for the physical, as I have already shown in the discussion on the miracles relating to the raising of the dead to life. This is clearly indicated by the words in which the message to John the Baptist is conveyed: "The blind receive their sight, and the lame walk, the lepers are cleansed, and the deaf hear, the dead are raised up, and the poor have the Gospel preached to them." And when the disciples of Jesus failed to turn out a devil, Jesus remarked: "This kind goeth not but by prayer and fasting."[36] It is by prayer and fasting that the power is attained to drive devils out of men, and clearly these are devils which affect the spirit and not the physique of man.

The light cast upon this subject by the Holy Qur'ān clears away all doubts. On three different occasions, the Holy Qur'ān is spoken of as a *Healing*: 10:57, 17:82 and 41:44. In fact, this is one of the names by which the Holy Book is known. The adoption of this name is a significant fact. It shows that the healing effected by the prophets of God is of a different nature from the removal of physical ailments. And again and again are the deaf and the dumb and the blind mentioned in the Holy Qur'ān; but these are not the armies of the sick by whom Jesus is supposed to have been followed: "And great multitudes followed him and he healed all",[37] Nay, the Holy Qur'ān itself tells us what it means by the blind and the deaf, etc.:

> They have hearts with which they do not understand, and they have eyes with which they do not see, and they have ears with which they do not hear.[38]

---

35. Art. "Gospels"   36. Matt. 17:21   37. Matt. 12:15   38. 7:179

For surely it is not the eyes that are blind, but blind are the hearts which are in the breasts.[39]

Similar statements abound in the Holy Qur'ān, but in view of the clearness and conclusiveness of what has been here quoted, I need not multiply instances. What is left obscure by the Gospels is thus made clear by the Holy Qur'ān and it is in this light that the Holy Book speaks of the healing effected by the prophets of God, of whom Jesus Christ is one.

4. Other Signs

Having disposed of the chief points in the miracles of Jesus, the raising of the dead and the healing of the sick, there is no need to dwell on the other wonderful works attributed to him. For instance, there is the miracle of turning water into wine recorded by St. John as his very first miracle. It is clearly an invention, for it does not behove a prophet of God to make people drunkards as Jesus is said to have done at the marriage feast of Cana. A prophet comes as a benefactor of humanity, and no one can be said to have done any good to fellow men who helps, by miracle or otherwise, in making men drunkards. But the Qur'ān, we are told, attributes to Jesus Christ two great miracles, *viz.* a possession of the knowledge of the unseen, and the power of creating life. And therefore it is necessary to say a few words about these.

Before we go to the Qur'ān, let us see, however, how far the Gospels lend colour to these claims. Now as regards the knowledge of the unseen, the Gospels do not furnish the least evidence. On the other hand, we are plainly told:

> But of that day and that hour knoweth no man, no, not the angels which are in heaven, neither the son, but the Father.[40]

---

39. 22:46
40. Mark 13:32

The knowledge of the unseen is here clearly disclaimed. Some knowledge of the future is revealed to the prophets of God, but unfortunately in the case of Jesus even the slight knowledge that was disclosed to him did not prove true according to the Gospels. He foretells his own second coming in the following words:

> For as the lightning cometh out of the east, and shineth even unto the west; so shall also the coming of the son of man be. For wheresoever the carcase is, there will the eagles be gathered together.

The commentators of the Gospels have been at great pains to explain this. We are told for instance that by the *carcase* is meant the sinful man and by the *eagles* Jesus Christ, though the singular form of the first and the plural of the second evidently leads to the opposite conclusion; but taking this explanation, it is very awkward that the coming of Jesus to sinners should be likened to the gathering of the vultures on a carcase. And then we are told:

> Immediately after the tribulation of those days shall the sun be darkened, and the moon shall not give her light, and the stars shall fall from heaven ... and then shall appear the sign of the Son of man in heaven. ... Verily I say unto you, this generation shall not pass, till all these things be fulfilled.[41]

That generation however passed away without witnessing the truth of these words and many more have followed. The promise failed, and the words of the Gospel shall always be the best comment on the Christian claim as to Jesus Christ's knowledge of the unseen. Blind faith needs no argument; nor is it shaken by argument; but the critical reader cannot find any explanation except that Jeus made a mistake in interpreting the prophecy. I say this in deference to Jesus' prophethood, though his own followers go far beyond that and declare the mistake to be due to Jesus' ignorance. The Rev. Dummelow says:

---

41. Matt. 24:27-34

Plumptre considers 'the boldest answer as the truest and most reverential,' and finds the explanation in Christ's *ignorance* of that day and hour.[42] Even if we assume, with Plumptre, complete ignorance of the date, we are no nearer a solution; for if he did not know the date, he would not attempt to fix it.

With such statements in the Gospels, he would be a very bold Christian who would proclaim to the world that Jesus had knowledge of the unseen. Even if the Holy Qur'ān had said what is ascribed to it, it does not seem befitting for a Christian to give the lie to his own sacred scriptures and to produce the Qur'ān, which he believes to be an imposture, in support of his statement. What he says to a Muslim is this: You must accept Jesus as being above a mortal because the Qur'ān says he had knowledge of the unseen, and when you have accepted him as such, you must believe in the Gospels and, on their basis, in the fact that he had no knowledge of the unseen. Could logic ever be more queer?

As regards the Holy Qur'ān, it nowhere speaks of Jesus Christ as having the the knowledge of the unseen. All that it says is this:

> And I inform you of what you should eat and what you should store in your houses.[43]

Here Jesus does not say that he knows what John ate last evening and what Peter left in his house which would be childish, but that he told people what they should eat and what they should store, and this was indeed what Jesus did when he said:

> Lay not up for yourselves treasures upon earth, where moth and rust doth corrupt, and where thieves break through and steal: But lay up for yourselves treasures in heaven, where neither moth nor rust doth corrupt and where thieves do not break through or steal for where your treasure is, there will your heart be also.[44]

And again:

---

42. Mark 13:32   43. 3:48   44. Matt. 6:19-21

Therefore take no thought, saying, what shall we eat? or,
What shall we drink? or, Wherewithal shall we be clothed?
... Take therefore no thought for the morrow; for the
morrow shall take thought for the things of itself.[45]

How well does the Christian world act up to these teachings!

The question of Jesus' knowledge of the unseen being thus
disposed of, there remains now the allegation that Jesus created
things. Had there been any truth in this, the Gospel writers who were
so much given to exaggeration that they transformed the ordinary
incidents of his life into wondrous deeds, would not have left this
unnoticed. Nor does the Holy Qur'ān anywhere call Jesus a creator.
On the other hand, it denies any such power in Jesus or any other
person or thing taken for a god. Thus it says:

Or have they set up with Allāh associates who have created
creation like His, so that what is created became confused to
them? Say: Allāh is the Creator of all things and He is the
One, the Supreme.[46]

This argument is as much against the divintiy of Jesus as of any other
person or thing, and the theory that the creation of certain things is
ascribed to Jesus by the Holy Qur'ān cannot stand for a moment
against this. This misunderstanding is due to two different
significances of the word _khalq_, the primary significance being
measuring, proportioning or _determining the measure_ or _proportion_
of a thing, while the other significance is _creating_. All the Arabic
lexicons agree on this; for facility I may refer the reader to Lane's
Arabic-English Lexicon. The word is extensively used in its primary
significance in Arabic literature, and Lane quotes several instances.
Thus _khalaq al-adīm-a_ means, _he measured_ or _proportioned the hide_,
khalaq an-na'l-a means, _he determined the measure of the sandal_,
and so on. It is in this sense that the commentators interpret the word
khalq as used about Jesus in 3:48, and even Lane accepts the same
interpretation, for he thus translates the words _inni akhluq-u lakum;_
"I will make according to its proper measure for you." The

---

45. 6:31, 34   46. 13:16

commentators of the Holy Qur'ān moreover say that the form thus proportioned did not actually turn into a bird: see the remark of *Wahb* quoted in the *Rūh al-Ma'āni*, that it was simply a momentary sight and the thing turned into dust immediately.

The performance at any rate, if really the form of a bird was made by Jesus, is far inferior to the grand miracle of Moses whose staff turned into a serpent. But it must be borne in mind that Jesus Christ spoke more in parables and metaphoric language than in plain words, and in this case too what he really meant was not the making of the figures of birds, a performance which had nothing to do with the work of a prophet, but the breathing of a spirit into his followers which should make them soar like birds in the higher spiritual regions.

Chapter 2

Sinlessness

Next to miracles, sinlessness is the most important argument of a Christian relating to the greatness of Jesus Christ. In fact, the very basis of the Christian religion is laid on the exclusive sinlessness of Jesus Christ. If Jesus Christ was not sinless or if any other person was sinless as well as Jesus, in both cases the Christian religion falls to the ground. The fundamental difference between Christianity and Islām is that the former teaches that every human child is born sinful, while the latter teaches that every human child is born sinless. According to the former, therefore, it would not avail a man to try to be good and perfect and to walk in the ways of truth and righteousness; for sin is inherent in human nature and man therefore can only be saved by the redemption of the Son of God. This view is so abhorrent in itself that it does not require to be refuted at any great length. That man is born sinful, or that sin is inherent in human nature, is to take the lowest possible view of human nature. No greater insult could be offered to humanity than to say that the new-born child was a sinful being. Yet on this is based the Christian doctrine that the child that dies before it is baptized shall burn in hell for the fault which can only be attributed to God Himself that He created him sinful. And if man is born sinful, and sin is therefore inherent in human nature, it is the height of absurdity to preach virtue to him and to tell him to shun every evil, for this in fact amounts to telling him that he should go against his nature. Such a doctrine could never have been conceived by him who believed in the innocence of little children:

> Suffer little children and forbid them not to come unto me, for of such is the kingdom of heaven.[47]

---

47. Matt. 19:14

30

Thus Christ himself taught the sanctity of childhood. But the Holy Prophet Muḥammad, may peace and the blessings of God be upon him, taught in clear words that "every child is born true to nature," i.e. sinless, and that he is a Muslim at his birth and "it is his parents that make him a Jew or a Christian or a Magian." And the Holy Qur'ān says in still plainer words:

> Then set your face upright for religion in the right state — the nature made by Allāh in which He has made men ... that is the right religion.[48]

Thus in Islām human nature is raised to the highest dignity by a plain declaration of its purity, while in Christianity it is brought down to the depth of degradation by declaring its inherent sinfulness, against which it is really impossible for it to go. This low view of human nature which forms the foundation-stone of the Christian religion must, sooner or later, be abandoned by the civilised world.

Not only does Islām start on the basis of the sinlessness of human nature and take its stand on the firm ground that every human child is born quite innocent, but it goes further and gives rules and regulations to keep up that inherent sinlessness. In the very first prayer taught by it, the prayer which is repeated five times a day by a Muslim, he is taught to aspire to sinlessness; nay far beyond that, to the great spiritual eminence to which arose the prophets and the truthful ones who were the greatest benefactors of humanity. Thus it says:

> Guide us on the right path, the path of those upon whom Thou hast bestowed favours.[49]

The chief distinction between the Muslim prayer and the Lord's prayer of the Christians is that while in the Lord's prayer forgiveness is sought for wrongs done, in the Muslim prayer man is taught to aspire to a place where wrong is not done at all, where not only evil is shunned but the greatest good is actually done. The former asks for forgiveness of sins, the latter for sinlessness, and for the doing of

---

48. 30:30   49. 1:5-6

good. Thus if, on the one hand, Islām elevates the dignity of human nature, on the other, it makes its aspirations to be the highest possible.

It is due to this fundamental difference between the two religions that Islām teaches the doctrine of the sinlessness of all the prophets of God, while Christianity inculcates the abhorrent doctrine that all the righteous men to whom humanity owes such a heavy debt of gratitude were sinful, and that Jesus alone, being more than a mortal, was sinless. Now, in the first place, it must be borne in mind that mere sinlessness is no proof of greatness. Sinlessness only implies the shunning of evil which is an inferior step in the progress of man to the doing of good, and it is on the measure of good which a man does that his greatness depends. We never ascribe greatness to a man simply because he has done harm to nobody; nay, it is the good which he does to humanity which entitles us to place him above the ordinary level. The question of sinlessness, therefore, on which the Christians lay so much stress, is one of very minor significance, while the real question is which prophet did the greatest amount of good to humanity. There may be, nay, there have been, hundreds of thousands of men who have passed their lives without doing any harm to anybody; they may have only been placed in circumstances in which they could not do any harm, or they may have chosen the life of a hermit, or living in the world they may have resisted its great temptations. Therefore for mere sinlessness, a man may not sometimes even deserve respect; at other times his conduct may be admirable; but in no case does he deserve to be called a great benefactor of humanity for merely avoiding to do harm to it. And the greatest benefactor of humanity, one who actually did the greatest amount of good to fellow-men is the great Prophet who is called "a mercy for the nations." He it is who did away with idolatry, who freed the world of the mighty demon of drink, who befriended the cause of the orphans, the poor and the weak, who established the principle of the equality of man, who did away with all invidious distinctions between race and race, who breathed a new spirit of union into the human race, who made knowledge take the place of ignorance, and who was a source of blessings to humanity in a thousand other ways.

However, we will take the question as put by a Christian. Is Jesus sinless? Are all the other prophets of God sinful? What does the Bible say on these two questions? What does the Holy Qur'ān say?

Let us take the Gospels first, and the question of the sinlessness of Jesus Christ. At the very commencement of his ministry he underwent a great temptation by the Devil. The events described there were not visible transactions but, as the commentators of the Gospels say, the "experience" of Jesus recorded in "symbolical language." This means in plain language that these were suggestions made to Jesus by the Devil, and this is inconsistent with the theory of his absolute sinlessness. The suggestion of the Devil is really the coming of an evil idea into man's heart, and though the idea may finally be rejected, even the first reception of it by the heart is inconsistent with the absolute purity of the mind. In the case of Jesus, however, three such evil thoughts occurred to him. The first suggestion of the Devil was made when Jesus was very hungry after a long fast: "Command that these stones be made bread".[50] The second was made by placing him on the pinnacle of a temple, or a *platform* as some would have it:

> Cast thyself down: for it is written, He shall give his angels charge concerning thee; and in their hands they shall bear thee up, lest at any time thou dash thy foot against a stone.[51]

The third was made by placing him on a high mountain from which "all the kingdoms of the world" and the glory of them was shown to him:

> All these things I will give to thee, if thou wilt fall down and worship me.[52]

This last was no doubt the culminating temptation and though Jesus rejected it with the significant words, "Thou shalt worship the Lord

---

50. Matt. 4:3   51. Matt. 4:6   52. Matt. 4:9

thy God, and him only shalt thou serve," the same cannot be said of his followers who have given themselves up to the worship of Mammon and the service of temporal glory to attain the self-same kingdoms. Here at any rate we have an incident which settles conclusively that Jesus did not possess absolute purity according to the Gospels, and the Devil could make suggestions to him as to any other human being. He had indeed the spiritual strength which enabled him to overcome the temptations, but if he had more of it, he would have been free from even the suggestions of the Devil. It may here be pointed out only by way of contrast that the Holy Qur'ān and the reports both speak of the Holy Prophet as having reached that highest stage of perfection where the Devil could not even make an evil suggestion to him, and it is to this that an authentic report refers according to which the Holy Prophet said that the Devil had become submissive to him, his actual words being: "Except that God has helped me against him so that he has submitted to me."

What is more important than this is that three of the Gospels contain a plain denial of sinlessness by Jesus himself. I quote the words from Mark:

> And when he was going forth into the way, there came one running and kneeled to him, and asked him, Good Master, what shall I do that I may inherit eternal life? And Jesus said unto him, Why callest thou me good? there is none good but one, that is, God.[53]

Now here Jesus is accosted as *good master* and if he had taken no objection, nobody could have drawn from it the conclusion that he claimed to be sinless. But he immediately rebukes the man for calling him *good*, for only *One*, that is God, is good. Why should he have taken objection to the use of the word *good* if he believed himself sinless? Nobody can tell; yet even so modern a commentator as the Rev. J.R. Dummelow makes the bold assertion that "this cannot mean that he was not good, but that for some reason or other on the present occasion he refused the title." What that reason was

---

53. Mark 10:17, 18

that being good he should still refuse to be called good and even give an argument why he could not be called good, nobody has ever been or shall ever be able to tell but the two explanations given had better have been omitted.

The first explanation is that the title *good* "in the sense in which it was offered" was unequal to his merits and his claims. He called him good "in the sense in which he would have called any eminent Rabbi good." A very bold suggestion! He was something more than *good* in the ordinary sense of that word and therefore he refused to be called *good*! But is this argument in conformity with the argument given by Jesus Christ himself? Had Jesus given no argument, such an explanation could have been invented, but when Jesus himself gives an argument it is very bold to ignore that argument and to invent one opposed to it. Jesus' argument is that *good* is a word which cannot be applied to any but God, and hence it cannot be applied even to him; in other words, his merits and his claims are unequal to the word *good*. But we are asked to accept just the opposite of it.

The other explanation is equally ludicrous: "The human nature of Christ, although sinless during the whole of of his earthly life, was not good in the absolute sense." This explanation would no doubt have been reasonable if Jesus Christ were looked upon as a mere mortal; it would in that sense have fitted in with the words, *for there is none good but one that is God.* But if Jesus was himself God, a Divine person, how could he refuse to be called *good* in the absolute sense, giving at the same time the reason that only God was good?

In fact, the words quoted above afford such clear and conclusive testimony against the doctrine of the sinlessness of Jesus that an attempt was made very early to tamper with the Gospels and to alter these words, but a change was made only in one of them. Thus in Matthew, while the Authorised Version is the same as in the other Gospels, the Revised Version introduces a change and puts the reply of Jesus in these words: "Why askest thou me concerning that which is good? One there is who is good." Little judiciousness seems to have been exercised in making this change, for the reply is very awkward in the mouth of Jesus. The man asked him as to what good he should do to have eternal life, and he says: "Why askest thou me concerning that which is good." This answer means either that he should have asked somebody other than Jesus concerning that which is good, or that he should have asked Jesus not concerning that which is good, but concerning that which is evil. That the change, however awkward, was made to escape the clear conclusion that Jesus was not sinless, is an admitted fact. The Rev. J.R. Dummelow says:

> The true version is clearly that of Mark and Luke. The author of Matthew (or perhaps an early scribe, for there is considerable reason for thinking that the original text of Matthew agreed with Mark and Luke) altered the text slightly, to prevent the reader from supposing that Christ denied that he was good.

The wish to do away with the words which were an obstacle in the way of establishing the sinlessness of Jesus may be looked upon by some as a pious one, but the act of altering the Holy Writ was no doubt one for which the Holy Qur'ān has rightly blamed the Christians.

If then the scriptures do not allow us to attribute at least absolute sinlessness to Jesus Christ, we will see whether they allow us to call the other prophets of God sinful. The following references from the Old Testament may first be considered. "Noah was a just man and perfect in his generations, and Noah walked with God."[54] To Abraham the Lord said: "Walk before me, and be thou perfect."[55] To Moses he said: "Thou shalt be perfect with the Lord thy God."[56] Can it be supposed that all these prophets were sinful notwithstanding their being perfect and their walking with God? Does not Jesus himself ask us to be perfect "even as your Father which is in heaven is perfect."[57] And what does perfection of the righteous servants of God mean except that they were sincere in heart, unblamable in life, innocent and harmless, and imitating God in doing good to others. In fact, *perfect* signifies much more than *sinless*. A man who is perfect in the sight of God is not only sinless

---

54. Gen. 6:9   55. Gen. 17:1   56. Deut. 18:13   57. Matt. 5:48

but also the doer of immense good. David thus speaks of the holy ones of God:

> Blessed are the perfect in the way who walk in the law of the Lord. Blessed are they that keep his testimonies, and that seek him with the whole heart. They also do no iniquity, they walk in his ways.[58]

And again:

> The mouth of the righteous speaketh wisdom, and his tongue talketh of judgment. The law of his God is in his heart; none of his steps shall slide.[59]

If the Old Testament thus speaks of the sinlessness of the prophets and the righteous ones in such clear words, the Gospels also give similar evidence. Testimony is borne to the sinlessness of Zacharias and his wife Elizabeth in the following words:

> And they were both righteous before God, walking in all the commandments and ordinances of the Lord blameless.[60]

If the doctrine of the sinlessness of Jesus can be based on the solitary words of St. John, "which of you convinceth me of sin," the clear words about Zacharias and Elizabeth that they were *blameless* certainly afford a firmer foundation for their sinlessness. For Jesus' only claim is that no man can accuse him of sin, but a man may be sinful in the eye of God though no human being may be able to accuse him of a sin. On the other hand, one whom God himself calls *blameless* is nothing if not sinless. it is for this reason that the child born of these two sinless parents is spoken of in the Gospels as being "filled with the Holy Ghost even from his mother's womb."[61] Now Jesus receives the Holy Ghost at thirty when he receives baptism at the hands of John the Baptist, but the Baptist is filled with the Holy Ghost from his mother's womb. Which of these two has the greater title to be called sinless?

A consideration of the Christian scriptures therefore shows conclusively that while they refuse to call Jesus sinless, they speak

---

58. Ps. 119:1-3   59. Ps. 37:30, 31   60. Luke 1:6   61. Luke 1:15

of other prophets of God and of His righteous servants as being
blameless and perfect. At any rate, the Christians have no ground, on
the basis of their scriptures, to ascribe any degree of sinlessness to
Jesus Christ which is not ascribable to other prophets. And now we
come to the Holy Qur'ān. The first question which we shall answer
here is: Does the Holy Qur'ān make any distinction between Jesus
Christ and the other prophets of God so far as the doctrine of
sinlessness is concerned? Not the least. All that can be said of Jesus
is that it speaks of him in kind words, but that is because the religion
of Islām is charitable towards other religions, and always speaks of
the other prophets in terms of the highest respect, the more so of
those who were abused at the time of its advent. It speaks of Jesus as
"a spirit from Him," not because it considers his nature to be Divine,
for it plainly speaks of him elsewhere as nothing more than a mortal,
but because his enemies abused him as having been illegitimately
born. The "spirit from God" in this case means only a pure soul, one
who is not the offspring of an illegal connection. God is the great
fountain-head of purity, and Jesus' soul is said to have come from
Him, meaning that it was a pure soul, and there was nothing of the
Devil in him as the Jews said when they called him illegitimate.

As regards the use of the word *Kalimatu-hu*, i.e. *His word*, there
is a misunderstanding. The meaning in this case simply is that he was
born according to a prophecy, according to the word which was
revealed to Mary, as the following quotation clearly shows:

> When the angels said, O Mary, surely Allāh gives you good
> news with a word from Him (of one) whose name is the
> Messiah, Jesus son of Mary.[62]

It would, however, be seen that the use of both the words
referred to above by no means entitles us to draw the conclusion that
Jesus was sinless. Is it not said of Adam:

> So when I have made him complete and breathed into him
> My spirit.[63]

---

62. 3:44   63. 15:29

And the same spirit that is breathed into Adam is breathed into everyone of his children:

> And He began the creation of man from dust. Then He made his progeny of an extract of water held in mean estimation. Then He made him complete and breathed into him of His spirit and made for you the ears and the eyes and the hearts.[64]

In both cases it is the false Christian doctrine which teaches that evil is innate in man that is refuted in describing the soul of Adam or the soul of every man as coming from God. The soul of Adam was pure by nature and so is the soul of every man, because it proceeds from a pure source, from God, the fountain-head of all purity, and evil is not inborn in the soul; in other words, there is no such thing as Original Sin. Every man that is born in this world, from Adam downwards, is born pure. It is only by his evil deeds that he makes the pure gift of God impure. By nature every man is pure; by his deeds he may become impure. And therefore no one is sinless simply because he is born sinless. The same is true of Jesus, and it is wrong to infer his sinlessness simply from the fact of his being called a "spirit from God." Every human soul is a spirit from God, but that does not carry us further than that he is born sinless. To show that he retains sinlessness, something more is needed.

Similarly, Jesus cannot be called sinless simply because he was born in accordance with a Divine prophecy. As a creature of God, he was a word of God; in fact, every creature of God is a word of God. The Qur'ān is very clear on this:

> If the sea were ink for the words of my Lord, the sea would surely be consumed before the words of my Lord are exhausted, though we were to bring the like of that sea to add thereto.[65]

And elsewhere the context makes it clear that by the words of God is meant only the creation of God:

---

64. 32:7-9   65. 18:109

What is in the heavens and the earth is Allāh's; surely Allāh
is the Self-sufficient, the Praised. And were every tree that
is in the earth made into pens and the sea to supply it with
ink, with seven more seas to increase it, the words of Allāh
would not come to an end; surely Allāh is Mighty, Wise.
Neither your creation nor your raising is anything but as a
single soul; surely Allāh is Hearing, Seeing.[66]

Jesus therefore enjoys no distinction in the claim to sinlessness by
being called a word of God.

The real question to be considered is, what does the Holy Qur'ān
say of his conduct in life? Does it say that he led his life in
sinlessness? Does it say that the other prophets did not lead their
lives in sinlessness? No such distinction is met with anywhere in the
pages of the Holy Book. All that is said of the conduct of Jesus is:

And to be kind to my mother; and He has not made me
insolent, unblessed.[67]

The Holy Qur'ān in these words only clears him of the charge of
insolence towards his mother which is implied in the incidents
narrated in the Gospels. But it speaks of other prophets in terms of
even higher praise. Thus it says of John, the Baptist:

And We granted him wisdom while yet a child, and
tenderness from Us and purity, and he was one who guarded
against evil, and dutiful to his parents, and he was not
insolent, disobedient.[68]

Now here we are plainly told not only that John was granted purity
but also that he was not disobedient, i.e. never committed a sin, and
thus he is plainly called sinless, an epithet not applied to Jesus Christ.
Is it not wonderful that the Holy Qur'ān mentions John and Jesus
together, and yet while it says of the one that he was sinless, of the
other it only says that he was not insolent to his mother? Why does
it not speak of Jesus also as being sinless? Does this omission imply
that the Holy Qur'ān did not look upon Jesus as a sinless person? Not

---

66. 31:26-28   67. 19:32   68. 19:12-14

at all. The truth is that what the Holy Qur'ān says of one prophet in such matters is true of all prophets. It is impossible that John should be sinless, while the other prophets are not sinless. But it has chosen John as a type in this case, and not Jesus, because the followers of Jesus had already gone so far as to raise him to the dignity of Godhead, and it its to warn them against their error that it does not speak of Jesus' conduct in the same commendatory words as of John's.

The pages of the Holy Qur'ān teem with such examples. Abraham is called *ṣiddīq* or *most truthful one*, but Jesus is not so called. Again, of him it is said that he was granted "direction," but the absence of such words in the case of other prophets does not imply that "direction" was not granted to them. Of Moses it is said:

> And I cast down upon you love from Me; and that you might be brought up before My eyes[69]

but other prophets had equally love cast down upon them from God though similar words have not been used about any of them anywhere in the Holy Qur'ān. It calls David *awwāb*, or one turning to God again and again, without meaning that the other prophets did not deserve to be called so. In fact, it treats all the prophets as one class, and when it speaks of one of them as possessing certain great qualities, it means that such great qualities are met with in all the other prophets. To this it directs attention in the following words:

> O apostles! eat of the good things and do good; surely I know what you do. And surely this your community is one community and I am your Lord.[70]

Hence it is that it speaks of the sinlessness of the prophets as a whole:

> And We did not send before you any apostle but We revealed to him that there is no God but Me, therefore serve Me. And they say, The Benificent God has taken to Himself a son; glory be to Him. Nay! they are honoured servants;

---

69. 20:39   70. 23:51, 52

they do not precede Him in speech and only according to His commandment do they act.[71]

Thus neither in word nor in deed do the prophets trespass the Divine limits, and this is conclusive proof that according to the Holy Qur'ān the prophets are sinless.

The Christian allegation against this is that while the Holy Prophet Muhammad is commanded to have recourse to *istighfār*, Jesus is not so commanded. Does it not show that the Holy Qur'ān accords a distinctive treatment to Jesus? The same mistake is made in this case. Noah, Hūd, Sālih, Shu'aib and others are equally not spoken of as resorting to *istighfār*. Does it show that these prophets were looked upon as sinless while the others were not regarded so? On the above mentioned grounds, no such distinction can be made between the various prophets. Nor does *istighfār* imply sinfulness. It denotes, on the other hand, the seeking of *ghafar* which word signifies, according to Rāghib, *the covering of a thing with that which will protect it from dirt*. Therefore *istighfār*, according to the best authority on the Qur'ānic lexicology, indicates simply the *seeking of a covering* or *protection*, a protection against chastisement as well as a protection against sins. Lane also explains *istaghfara* as meaning *he sought of God covering* or *forgiveness* or *pardon*. Qastalānī, one of the commentators of *Bukhārī*, says *ghafar* means *sitr*, i.e. *covering*, and it is either between man and his sin or between sin and its punishment. It will thus be seen that the idea of *protection* or *covering* is the dominant idea in *ghafar* and *istighfār*, and these words therefore signify *protection against sins* as well as *protection against punishment*. They include two cases: (1) as against a fault that has been committed, protection from punishment; and (2) as against a fault not committed but to which man as man is liable, protection from the commission of it. The words are used in the Holy Qur'ān in both senses. I give here only one instance of the second significance. At the end of the second chapter a prayer is taught: "And pardon us and grant us protection and have mercy on us." The

---

71. 21:25-27

original word for *grant us protection* is *ighfir lanā*, which if rendered as *pardon us* becomes meaningless for that significance is conveyed by the previous word *wa'fu'-'annā*. Three distinct things are here plainly prayed for, viz.: (1) pardon for sins already committed; (2) protection from sin to which one is liable; and (3) mercy or favour from God.

As I have already shown, since the Holy Qur'ān has established in plain words the principle of the sinlessness of prophets, *istighfār* in their case can only be taken as meaning *the seeking of protection from the sins to which man is liable*, and in this sense all the prophets of God and all righteous men resort to *istighfār* i.e. they ply for protection to God. *Istighfār* in this sense is the best means of attaining to sinlessness. The man who trusts in his own strength in the struggle against the evil one is sure to fall; therefore the righteous servants of God ply for protection to Allāh, and there under divine protection they are perfectly safe. *Istighfār* in this sense really makes a man attain to the highest stage of spiritual progress, and therefore the prophets of God who all attain to that stage have always recourse to it. And if some prophets are not mentioned as resorting to *istighfār*, at least the angels are spoken of as doing *istighfār* for all of them. Thus in 40:7, the angels are shown as praying for the righteous in the following words: "Grant protection to those who turn to Thee and follow Thy way," where in the original the word *ighfir* is used. Now all the prophets of God, and Jesus among them, must be included among those who "follow Thy way," and this verse therefore shows that *istighfār* is not only resorted to by the righteous themselves but also by the angels of God for their sake. And in the case of Jesus, his grandmother is mentioned as praying for him long before his birth in similar words: "And I have named it Mary and I commend her and her offspring into Thy protection from the accursed devil",[72] where *i'āzah* is used instead of *istighfār*, the significance of both words being the same.

---

72. 3:35

Before leaving this subject, however, it seems necessary to throw light on one more point. It is sometimes said that the Prophet is commanded to do *istighfār* for his *dhanb* which means *sin*. Even if *sin* were taken to be the meaning of *dhanb*, the significance would be that he should seek Divine protection from the *dhanb* to which as a human being he was liable. But really *dhanb* is a term conveying a very wide significance and does not always indicate a *sin*. Rāghib tells us that *dhanb* is originally *the taking the tail of a thing, and it is applied to every act of which the consequence is disagreeable* or *unwholesome*. According to Lane, *dhanb* means *a sin, a crime, a fault*. It is said to differ from *ithm*, in being either intentional or committed through inadvertence, whereas *ithm* is particularly intentional (see Lane's *Lexicon* which has quoted authorities). It will thus be seen that *dhanb* is a word which carries a very wide significance and is applicable as well to sins due to perversity as to shortcomings resulting from inattention, and even to defects and imperfections of which the result may be disagreeable; and the use of this word in the Holy Qur'ān, where it is applied to all shades of shortcomings, from the grossest transgressions of the wicked to those defects and imperfections of human nature from which even the most perfect mortal cannot be free, is quite in accordance with the lexicons. In the English language the word *sin* is therefore by no means the equivalent of *dhanb*, and the word *fault* makes the nearest approach to its wide significance.

We are sometimes told by irresponsible Christian controversialists that the Holy Prophet Muhammad worshipped idols in his childhood and that he is therefore called *an erring one* in the Holy Qur'ān. This is a statement for which there is not the least evidence. On the other hand, there is sure historical testimony that, as early as his journey to Syria in the company of his uncle, he expressed his strong hatred for idol-worship, so that when two idols were named before him, he cried out: "By Allāh! I have never hated anything with the hatred which I entertain towards them." Of his childhood, many anecdotes are related by his uncle, Abū Ṭālib, whose great affection for the Prophet, for the great qualities which he found in him, withstood the oppostion of the whole of his nation later on, when the Quraish rose up against him to a man, and these afford strong evidence of his abhorrence of idol-worship and everything mean. Abū Ṭālib told his brother 'Abbās that he never found Muhammad, may peace and the blessings of God be upon him, telling a lie, nor did he ever witness in him derisiveness or ignorance (a general term for everything bad); nor did he ever go out with children taking part in their sports. Not only there was nothing mean or low ever witnessed in him, but honesty, veracity and other great qualities were met with in him to so great an extent that he earned the honourable name of al-Amīn, i.e. *the honest one*, among his compatriots.

The Holy Qur'ān nowhere describes him as one erring. On the other hand, it says plainly: "Your companion did not err, nor did he deviate."[73] The word *ḍāll* does not always signify one *erring*. Lane tells us that the verb *ḍalla* of which *ḍāll* is the nominative form signifies *he was perplexed and unable to see the way*. It is this significance which is conveyed by the word *ḍāll* in 93:7, as the context clearly shows. There we have first three statements:

> Did He not find you an orphan and give thee shelter? And find you unable to see the way and show it? And find you in want and make you to be free from want?

and corresponding to each of these statements respectively and in the same order, we have then three injunctions:

> Therefore as for the orphan, do not oppress him. And as for him who asks, do not chide him. And as for the favour of your Lord, do announce it.

This will make it clear that as in the first statement, we have the Holy Prophet described as an orphan, accordingly the first injunction is that the orphans should not be oppressed. And as in the third statement we have the Holy Prophet described as being in want whom Divine favour made free of want, accordingly the third injunction is that he should announce these favours to the world.

---

73. 53:2

This arrangement makes it certain that the second statement and the second injunction must also correspond with each other. Now the second injunction is clear. It says that one who asks about a thing should not be chided, while the second statement says that the Prophet was guided after being found in a certain state. The correspondence between the two makes it certain that the state was the state of one who asks about religious truths, because the consequence is that he is guided aright. Thus the fact stated is that the Holy Prophet, finding those around him in a degenerate state, was anxious to reform them, but was unable to find out the path by treading which he could bring about the regeneration, and it was God Who guided him into that path. Allāh found the Prophet in quest of the way, but as he was unable to chalk out a way for himself, He guided him by Divine light. And the Holy Qur'ān explains itself when it says elsewhere: "And thus did We reveal to you an inspired Book by Our command; you did not know what the Book was, nor what the faith was, but We made it a light guiding thereby whom We please of Our servants."[74]

---

74. 42:52

Chapter 3

Circumstances Relating to Birth

1. Announcement of Birth

The next chain of arguments is connected with the circumstances relating to the birth of Jesus and the Holy Prophet Muḥammad. The foremost ground among these is occupied by the fact of the announcement of birth. The argument runs thus: "The miraculous nature of the birth of Christ is evident from the Qur'ān. The good news of it was given to Mary through Gabriel. As against this the birth of Ḥaḍrat Muḥammad is not so much as mentioned in the Qur'ān. His birth was neither miraculous, nor extraordinary. Therefore in respect of birth, Christ, son of Mary, is superior to Muḥammad."

This argument consist of two parts; viz.: (1) that the birth of Christ was miraculous, and (2) that the good news of it was given to Mary. Let us take the first part. What is meant by miraculous has not been explained at all, nor has any verse of the Holy Qur'ān been quoted. The Holy Book speaks of Jesus as having been born like ordinary human children. A plain description of it is given in the chapter entitled Mary:

> Then she conceived him, then withdrew herself with him to a remote place. And the throes of childbirth compelled her to betake herself to the trunk of a palm-tree. She said: O

47

would that I had died before this and had been a thing quite forgotten.[75]

This shows clearly that Mary conceived Jesus in the ordinary way in which women conceive children and she gave birth to him in the usual manner in which women give birth to children. There is nothing miraculous, nothing extraordinary in the conception and in the birth. There is no verse in the Holy Qur'ān stating that Mary conceived Jesus by the Holy Ghost. Even the Holy Prophet is said to have silenced the Christian deputation of Najrān by saying:

> Surely Jesus — his mother conceived him in the same manner as a women conceives, and she gave birth to him in the same manner as a woman gives birth to her child, then he was given food in the same manner as a baby is given food.[76]

Was Jesus conceived without the intervention of a male parent? The Holy Qur'ān, as I have said, does not answer this question in the affirmative, neither is there any saying of the Holy Prophet on record containing such an assertion. Nor is it a point on which the whole Muslim world agrees. There are some who answer the above question in the negative; others who do so in the affirmative. We will take first the latter view. Even if we suppose Jesus to have been born without the intervention of a male parent, this abnormality gives us no ground to consider him superior to those prophets who while doing immensely greater work were born in the ordinary course of nature. The ordinary human mind cannot conceive how an abnormal condition in the birth of a man makes him superior to others. Of course if it is to be believed only like the Atonement and the Trinity, that question cannot be asked, but if it is put forward as an *argument*, the case must be argued and it must be explained what high qualities and Divine attributes which men born in the ordinary course of nature could not possess, were the natural outcome of this abnormality. I call it only an abnormal condition from a Muslim's point of view because no Muslim believes that the Holy Ghost had

---

75. 19:22, 23   76. *Rūh al-Ma'ānī*, chapter 3

taken the place of the male parent, and because it could neither be the miracle of Jesus who was not yet born, nor that of Mary who was not a prophetess and who had not been raised for the regeneration of the Israelite nation.

A miracle moreover is an act which takes place before the public, and it is needed to satisfy and convince others; but both these elements are absent in this case. How could anybody in the world possibly know that Mary had conceived a child without intercourse with a male being? If in fact she conceived him thus extraordinarily, it could serve as a miracle for *her and for her alone*. And who would accept her statement in this matter when she could not produce a single witness? Nay, instead of satisfying and convincing, it could only raise further serious doubts as to the truth of the prophethood of Jesus. There does not therefore exist the least justification for calling that a miracle of which no one in the world could at all have direct information. Even Mary's husband, a just man, was, according to the Gospel, determined "to put her away privately," refraining on account of pity on her, from making "her a public example"[77], had it not been for the vision he saw afterwards, and thus even in his case it was the vision which satisfied him and not the conception, and therefore the vision, not the conception, served the purpose of a miracle in his case. But, evidently, the Jews did not see similar visions, and so there was no miracle for them. The alleged extraordinary conception was therefore only an abnormal condition, and if it really took place in this manner, it was only a sign that the last of the great line of the Israelite prophets had come into the world and that prophethood would now shift to the sons of Ishmael, the other great line of Abraham's descendants with whom the covenant was made.

Call it what we may, being brought into the world only through a woman — and not the union of man and woman — is no evidence of excellence. If this peculiar way of advent into life does entitle a person to superiority, Adam must be held to be the most excellent

---

77. Matt. 1:19

human being, and far superior to Jesus Christ, because he came into life without the agency of either parent. Nay, even Eve was superior to Jesus Christ because she too came into life in the same manner — at any rate she was made from man, and as man is superior to woman, so must Eve be superior to Christ. And the most wonderful of all is Melchisedec of Gen. 14, whose priesthood was recognised even by Abraham.

For this Melchisedec, king of Salem, priest of the most High God, who met Abraham returning from the slaughter of the kings and blessed him ... without father, without mother, without descent, having neither beginning of days, nor end of life, but made like unto the Son of God; abideth a priest continually'[78].

To say that "without father" means that his father is not mentioned in the Bible and that "having neither beginning of days, nor end of life" signifies that the Bible does not say when he was born and when he died, is not only to play with words, but also to betray ignorance of what Paul says clearly that he was "made like unto the Son of God." At any rate Adam, Eve, and Melchisedec must be recognised as possessors of a far greater degree of excellence than Jesus Christ if being born without a father is any criterion of greatness.

If we, however, go to the root of the question we find, that the Holy Qur'ān nowhere speaks of Jesus having been conceived miraculously, nor is the statement anywhere contained in it that Jesus had no father. In the absence of any clear and conclusive statement either in the Holy Qur'ān or in the reports narrated from the Holy Prophet, we are left to certain inferences from certain words of the Qur'ān, and it is these that I shall now discuss briefly. The greatest stress is laid on the point that when the good news of a son was announced to Mary, she exclaimed: "My Lord! How shall there be a son born to me and man has not touched me." And the reply thereto is: "Even so; Allāh creates what He pleases; when He has decreed a matter, He only says to it, Be, and it is"[79]. The inference drawn

---

78. Heb. 7:1-3   79. 3:46

from this question and answer is that a promise was given that she would conceive without a man ever touching her. Now this inference is not correct. For when similar news was announced to Zacharias, he cried out: "My Lord, how shall there be a son born to me and old age has already come upon me and my wife is barren?" And the reply thereto is: "Even so; Allāh does what He pleases".[80] The same word *Kadhālika* is used to impress the fact that the matter had been ordained thus and must take place. As "even so" in the latter case does not signify that a son would be born in spite of Zacharias' wife remaining barren, so the same word in the case of Mary does not signify that a son would be born to her in spite of the fact that man shall not have touched her. The words "even so" in both cases are introduced to emphasise the assurance given to make it known that what has been said shall take place by all means.

The Holy Qur'ān does not lend any support to the view that the vow of Mary's mother to devote her to Divine service implied anything like a vow of celibacy, for while making the vow she speaks in clear words of Mary's children: "And I commend her and her offspring into Thy protection".[81] The words *her offspring* clearly show that Mary's mother in spite of the vow knew that she should marry and have children like any other woman in the world.

This conclusion which in fact upsets the whole theory of the miraculous conception is corroborated by what is stated in the Gospels. The life of Mary as depicted there clearly shows her to be a woman living with her husband in the ordinary relations of husband and wife. In the very first chapter of Matt. we read:

> Then Joseph being raised from the sleep did as the angel of the Lord had bidden him, and took unto him his wife; and knew her not till she had brought forth her first-born son.[82]

"Joseph knew her not till she had brought forth" is too clear to need any comment; it clearly shows that the writer means that after the birth of Jesus, Joseph and Mary lived as husband and wife. Other statements in the Gospels clearly show that not only did Joseph and

---

80. 3:39   81. 3:35   82. vv. 24 and 25

Mary live as husband and wife, but they were blessed with a number
of children, the brothers and sisters of Jesus Christ:

> When he yet talked to the people, behold his mother and his
> brethren stood without, desiring to speak with him. Then one
> said unto him, Behold thy mother and thy brethren stand
> without.[83]

And a little further on:

> And when he was come into his own country, he taught
> them in the synagogue, in so much that they were
> astonished, and said, Whence hath this man this wisdom,
> and these mighty works? Is not this the carpenter's son? Is
> not his mother called Mary? and his brethren, James and
> Joseph and Simon and Judas? And his sister, are they not all
> with us?.[84]

And in Luke 2:7, Jesus is called Mary's first-born son, not her only
son, showing clearly that she had other offspring. From this it is clear
that not only did Joseph and Mary live together as husband and wife
but that they had many other children besides Jesus Christ as it is to
this that the Holy Qur'ān refers in the words *her offspring*.

In the same connection it may be noted that it is equally wrong
to draw an inference of Mary's celibacy from the words, "and Mary,
the daughter of 'Amrān, who guarded her chastity" occurring in the
chapter entitled *Tahrīm*.[85] Every woman who is married and lives
with her husband in fact guards her chastity and is for this reason that
the Holy Qur'ān speaks of married women as *muhsanāt* or those
guarding their chastity. These words are only a refutation of the
Jewish calumny against Mary.

Why is Jesus called the son of Mary if he had a male parent? The
answer to this question is that his description as the son of a woman
is really meant as a refutation of his divinity. The foundation of the
Christian religion rests on the assumption that sin was brought into
the world by a woman. Strangely enough, when the Christians

---

83. Matt. 12:46, 47 84. Matt. 13:54-56 85. 66:12

thought of doing away with the need of one of the parents in the case of Jesus to make him divine, they made a wrong choice. They did away with the male parent and kept the woman, the real source of sin according to them. "How can he be clear that is born of a woman".[86] Such being the verdict of the sacred scriptures of the Christians, the *son of Mary* cannot be raised to the dignity of Godhead and it is of this that the Holy Qur'ān reminds them again and again in speaking of Jesus as *son of Mary*. Moreover where the mother is the more celebrated of the parents, it is only natural that her name should receive a preference. Mary being a sacred and righteous woman, Jesus is called *her* son and not of Joseph, an ordinary carpenter, to whose sanctity of character even the Gospels bear no witness.

Much stress is sometimes laid on the fact that the Holy Qur'ān refers to the calumnies of the Jews against Mary. It is asserted that such calumnies would not have existed if Mary had had a husband when Jesus was born. This inference is very far-fetched. That Mary had a husband is shown by the Gospels where the life-story of Jesus is recorded. In Gospels too Jesus is called "the carpenter's son." Therefore the calumnies referred to in the Holy Qur'ān must relate to something other than the relations of Joseph and Mary who were known to be husband and wife. The truth is that the Jews, in order to denounce both Mary and her son, falsely accused her of adultery, and it is to this accusation that the Holy Qur'ān refers and it is against this that the Holy Book defends Mary. The assertion that only an unmarried woman could be accused of illicit intercourse is the strangest of all.

The question of the miraculous birth being thus disposed of, we now come to the second part of the argument, viz. that the good news of the birth of Jesus was given to Mary while the news of the birth of the Holy Prophet Muḥammad, on whom be peace, was not announced to his mother. Not even the drowning man would catch at such straws as otherwise sensible men sometimes do in their

---

86. Job. 25:4

religious zeal. Is it true that when the birth of a child is announced to a parent by way of prophecy, the child becomes the possessor of great qualities and is raised to a dignity to which others are not raised? If so, thousands of fathers and mothers in the world see visions as to the birth of children, and all these children would be equal rank with Jesus — would they all be more than mortal as Jesus is believed to be? And what are we to think of John the Baptist, the good news of whose birth was announced prophetically to his father, and who comes first when the birth of Jesus is spoken of, not only in the Holy Qur'ān but also in the Gospels? In this respect, then, even John can claim equality with, if not precedence over Jesus.

For the father or the mother to see a vision that a son would be born to him or her is the most ordinary thing and is not the least evidence of the greatness of the offspring. Such a vision does not in itself show that the child whose advent has been foretold would accomplish some great purpose in the world. On the other hand, when the advent of a prophet is foretold through another prophet, there is a clear suggestion that the prophet whose appearance is thus announced to the world long before is the possessor of some great and mighty excellence, and the world is in fact beforehand told that it must await the great day. Hence it is that the Holy Qur'ān, the Book of Wisdom as it is, does not speak of the vision seen by the Holy Prophet's mother, though historically it is beyond all doubt that she saw such a vision: "I am the vision of my mother," being the words of the Holy Prophet himself; but it lays great emphasis on the prophecies speaking of the advent of the Holy Prophet as met with in the previous Scriptures or as made by the previous prophets. Thus it has in a Mecca revelation: "And most surely the same is in the Scriptures of the ancients",[87] where it is clearly asserted that prophecies of the advent of the Holy Prophet are to be met with in all the ancient Scriptures. This is stated still more clearly and in a more emphatic tone in a later revelation: "And when Allāh made a covenant through the prophets: certainly what I have given you of book and wisdom — then an Apostle comes to you verifying that

---

87. 26:196

which is with you, you must believe in him and you must aid him. He said: Do you affirm and accept My compact in this matter? They said, We do affirm"[88]. This verse lays down in the clearest and strongest words that all the prophets had foretold the advent of the great World-Prophet and laid an obligation upon their followers to accept him, while he on his part required a belief in all the prophets that had gone before him. Here then we have not one woman, the mother of the child, who receives the good news of the advent of our Holy Prophet, but the best minds in all the nations of the world, the greatest benefactors of the whole human race, whenever and wherever they lived, received the cheering news, the mighty announcement, that the nations of the world would not live enstranged from each other looking always to different guides, but they would all be united in the World-Prophet whose great sign was that he would testify to the truth of all the previous prophets. Turn over the pages of all the sacred Scriptures of the world, and you will find only One book, the Holy Qur'ān, which requires a belief in all the previous revelations, and read over the histories of all the great reformers of the world and you will find only One Man, the Holy Prophet Muḥammad, who required his followers to accept all the prophets of the world. Thus the Holy Qur'ān shows unmistakably that Muḥammad, may peace and the blessings of God be upon him, was the Great Prophet, about whom all the prophets prophesied, and in whom centred all the great hopes of the whole world. And not only the Holy Qur'ān but even the Bible leads us to the same conclusion, as we read in Acts 3:21-22:

> Whom the heaven must receive until the time of the restitution of all things, which God hath spoken by the mouth of all his holy prophets since the world began. For Moses truly said unto the fathers, A prophet shall the Lord your God raise up unto you of your brethren, like unto me; him shall ye hear in all things whatsoever he shall say unto you.

---

88. 3:80

The Christians think that the prophet spoken of here is Jesus Christ, but the decisive factor in this statement is that the prophet about whom all the prophets prophesied is the promised one of Deut. 18:18, and that prophecy applies only to the Holy Prophet Muhammad and to none else.

"The Apostle-Prophet, the *Ummi*, whom they find written down with them in the Torah and the Gospel."[89] These words of the Holy Qur'ān affirm that prophecies of the same, one prophet, are met with both in the Torah and the Gospel, and they are no doubt a bold challenge to the followers of Moses and Christ, the more so when it is borne in mind that the challenge is put into the mouth of one who never read either books of Moses or the Gospels, of the *Ummi* prophet, as he is plainly called here, the resident of the metropolis of Arabia, who did not know reading or writing. That both the Torah and the Gospel contain a prophecy of the advent of one and the same prophet, and that that Prophet is no other than Muhammad, may peace and the blessings of God be upon him, are two very significant claims made by the Holy Qur'ān, and the conclusive evidence afforded by them of the truth of the Holy Prophet is one of the greatest miracles that the world has ever witnessed.

The prophecy of Moses runs thus: "I will raise them up a Prophet from among their brethren, like unto thee, and will put my words in his mouth."[90] Hundreds of years pass away until we come to the time of Jesus Christ and find it again recorded in clear words that the Promised Prophet of Deuteronomy had not yet made his appearance. John the Baptist claimed to be a prophet a little before Jesus and being asked, "he confessed and denied not; but confessed, I am not the Christ. And they asked him, What then? Art thou Elias? And he saith, I am not. Art thou that prophet? And he answered, No."[91]

We know that the Jews expected a Messiah, and hence they asked John if he was Christ. We know further that they had been told that the Prophet Elias would come again and hence their second question. But who is "that prophet" about whom they ask in the last

---

89. 7:157   90. Deut. 18:18   91. John 1:20-21

instance? Evidently, it must be a prophet who had been promised to them, and such was only the promised prophet of Deut. 18:18. This is not a mere conjecture but the decided opinion of the Christians themselves, for in the margin of an ordinary Bible giving references we find in a note on the words "that prophet" a reference to Deut. 18:15, 18. This settles the point conclusively: the Promised Prophet of Deuteronomy had not yet appeared. But while the Gospels make it plain that in John the Baptist was fulfilled the promise of the return of Elias, and Jesus claimed to be the Christ, none of them ever claimed to be the Promised Prophet of Deuteronomy. Thus it is established conclusively by the Gospels that the Promised Prophet of Deuteronomy had not appeared up to the advent of John and Jesus and that neither John nor Jesus was that prophet. The claim of the Holy Prophet Muḥammad to be the Promised Prophet "whom they find written down with them in the Torah and the Gospel" is thus uncontested, and no Jew or Christian can deny this truth unless he belies his own books.

The Gospel, however, is still more clear. If St. John has preserved for us the fact that expectations of the Promised Prophet were not fulfilled till the time of Jesus, nor yet in John and Jesus, he has also preserved the prophecy of Christ about the advent of that great Deliverer:

> And I will pray the Father, and He shall give you another Comforter, that he may abide with you for ever.[92]

And again:

> It is expedient for you that I go away: for if I go not away, the Comforter will not come unto you.[93]

And further again:

> Howbeit when he, the Spirit of Truth, is come, he will guide you into all truth.[94]

This other Comforter, this Spirit of Truth who was to guide men "into all truth," was no other than the Promised Prophet of

---

92. John 14:16-17 93. John 14:7 94. John 14:13

Deuteronomy, no other than the Holy Prophet Muḥammad, may peace and the blessings of God be upon him, the *Truth* with whose advent falsehood vanished,[95] the greatest and the last Prophet of the world with whom religion was brought to perfection.[96]

The two prophecies, the prophecy of Moses foretelling the appearance of one like him, and the prophecy of Jesus giving the world the good news of the appearance of another Comforter who should be the last Prophet of the world and whose Law should be a perfect Law, guiding "into all truth," are a magnificent testimony to the greatness of the Holy Prophet Muḥammad, and the Holy Qur'ān draws attention to these two prophecies in particular. In 73:15, it clearly speaks of the Prophet's likeness to Moses:

> Surely We have sent to you an Apostle, a bearer of witness to you, *as* We sent an apostle to Pharaoh

and in 61:6, it plainly states that the Holy Prophet was the Comforter whose good news was given by Jesus:

> And when Jesus son of Mary said: O children of Israel, surely I am the apostle of Allāh to you, verifying that which is before me of the Torah, and giving the good news of an Apostle who will come after me, his name being Aḥmad.

It must be remembered that the Holy Prophet was known by both the names Muḥammad and Aḥmad from his very childhood, both names being given to him at his birth. It would thus be seen that it is a very poor argument of the greatness of Jesus Christ and of his superiority to the Holy Prophet Muḥammad, may peace and the blessings of God be upon him, that the birth of Jesus was announced to his mother in a vision.

Of all the prophets of the world, the Holy Prophet of Islam alone has the unimaginably high distinction of having come in fulfilment of the visions of all the prophets of the world and the Holy Qur'ān,

---

95. "The Truth has come and the falsehood vanished; surely falsehood is a vanishing thing" (17:81).
96. "This day have I perfected for you your religion and completed My favour on you and chosen for you Islām as a religion" (5:3).

having mentioned this mighty argument of his greatness and superiority above all, very wisely omits the mention of his mother's vision, a matter of secondary importance in comparison with the great news which it had announced.

2. Mother's Greatness

Another argument in the same connection runs thus:

> The Qur'ān itself has mentioned the excellence of Mary, the mother of Christ, above the women of the world and has given her the title of *Ṣiddīqah* (the righteous woman). But the very name of Ḥaḍrat Muḥammad's mother is not to be met with in the Qur'ān and some Muslims do not hold her to be a believer. From this also it appears that Christ, the son of Mary, is greater than Ḥaḍrat Muḥammad.

Because the mother is a great woman, her son must also be a great man; such in simple words is the logic of the writer! But how did the mother become great if her mother again was not a great woman? And continue this to Eve, the first female parent of the human race: she must be at least as great as Mary. According to this Christian argument, therefore, Mary's greatness not only imparts that greatness to Jesus and *his brothers and sisters*, but this logic makes Eve and her offspring — the whole human race — to be as great as Jesus Christ.

The real question for a Christian however is: What do the Gospels say about "the mother of God" and her greatness? From his point of view, the truth is in the Gospels and what is against a Gospel statement cannot be used as an argument against an adversary. If the Gospels give her the same place of honour as the Qur'ān does, it is good to produce the Qur'ānic testimony, but if they treat her as an ordinary woman, it is illogical for a Christian to seek shelter in the Qur'ānic statements. Now what do the Gospels say?

> Then one said unto him, Behold, thy mother and thy brethren stand without, desiring to speak with thee. But he

answered and said unto him that told him, Who is my
mother? and who are my brethren? And he stretched forth
his hand toward his disciples, and said, Behold my mother
and my brethren! For whosoever shall do the will of my
Father which is in heaven, the same is my brother, and sister,
and mother.[97]

This incident is recorded by all the synoptists in almost the same
words, Mark 3:31-35 and Luke 8:19-21, the concluding words of
Luke running thus: "My mother and my brethren are these which
hear the word of God, and do it." What does this show? The
conclusion is inevitable that according to the Gospels, Jesus' mother
did not believe in his message. Even if she had been an ordinary
believer and not the great woman which the Christians try to make
her, Jesus would not have spoken of her in these insulting words:
Who is my mother? She stood without to speak with Jesus, but Jesus
did neither go out to meet her, nor did he send her word to come in
and sit with the disciples. If she had been a believer in Jesus, she
could at least have taken her place with the disciples, with those who
were sitting there to learn something from the Master. But Jesus
considers her to be unworthy of that company. Not only that, but he
also plainly told the informant that his mother and his brethren were
those that did the will of the heavenly Father, those that heard the
word of God and did it, and to leave no doubt on the point, pointed
to the disciples as answering that description, leaving intentionally
the mother and the brethren. On another occasion Jesus is said to
have addressed his mother thus: "Woman, what have I to do with
thee?".[98]

The Gospels, therefore, instead of representing Mary as a great
woman, describe her in words which make it probable that she was
not even a believer in the message of Jesus Christ, and this view was
no doubt taken by the writers of the Gospels. The Jews, on the other
hand, circulated calumnies of all sorts against her and depicted her
character as that of a fallen woman. As it was one of the objects of

97. Matt. 12:47-50 98. John 2:4

the Qur'ān to inculcate respect for all righteous men and women, and Mary and her son were among the most, if not *the* most, reviled of all the holy personages in the world, it was bound to defend them. The Jews said that Mary was among the most degraded women of her time; the Holy Qur'ān tells us that she was the greatest woman of her time, pure and chaste. Thus it says:

> And when the angels said, O Mary! Surely Allāh has chosen you and purified you and chosen you above the women of the world.[99]

The words being a reproduction of how the angels then addressed Mary show that what was implied was the excellence of Mary over the women of her time, and not the women of all times and ages. Only a few verses above the passage we have a similar description of Adam and Noah and the descendants of Abraham and the descendants of 'Imrān: "Surely Allāh chose Adam and Noah and the descendants of 'Imrān above the world."[100] Exactly the same words *istifā* and *'ālamīn* are used here as in the case of Mary. Can it then be supposed that the Holy Qur'ān speaks of granting excellence to all these people above the world for all times? Adam was chosen above the world, Noah was chosen above the world, the descendants of Abraham were chosen above the world, the descendants of 'Imrān were chosen above the world, and lastly Mary was chosen above the women of the world.

Everyone can see that if we put upon these words the wide interpretation which a Christian puts upon the passage speaking of Mary, the whole becomes contradictory in itself. But if we limit the meaning of *'ālamīn* to the world as existing then, to the people of the time, the meaning is clear. Adam was the greatest man of his time; Noah was the greatest man of his time; the descendants of Abraham were the most excellent nation of their day; the descendants of 'Imrān were the greatest people of their age; and Mary was the greatest woman of those living in her time. It is thus that the commentators have explained the words spoken regarding the whole

---

99. 3:41   100. 3:32

Israelite nation: "I made you excel the world"[101], because the same Israelite nation is spoken of in the Holy Qur'ān as having made itself deserving of Divine wrath.[102]

Similarly, the title of *siddīqah* was given to Mary by the Holy Qur'ān to show that the Gospels did not record the facts truly and that the implied charge against Mary that she was not a believer in the message of Jesus Christ was wrong. The word *siddīq* (of which *siddīqah* is the feminine form) properly means *one who is truthful in the highest degree* and is applied to one who is a firm believer in the truth of Divine messages. Thus the Holy Qur'ān says:

> And as for those who believe in Allāh and His apostles, these it is that are the truthful (Ar. *siddīqah*), and the faithful ones in the sight of their Lord.[103]

Thus by calling Mary a *siddīqah*, the Holy Qur'ān only shows that the Gospels in our hands have misrepresented the facts. As regards the title of *siddīq* or *siddīqah*, if the Holy Qur'ān gives it to Mary, it also gives it to every true follower of the Holy Prophet Muhammad, as shown by the above quotation. And *siddīqah* was the title of 'Ā'isha, the wife of the Holy Prophet, who enjoys the distinction of being a *siddīqah* to such a high degree that that epithet has not only become a part of her name, 'Ā'isha siddīqah, but even when used alone, it stands for her.

As to the assertion that the Holy Prophet's mother was an unbeliever, it is sufficient to note that she died when he was yet six years old, while he was called to the office of prophet when he was forty years of age. How could she then be said to be an unbeliever? Our Holy Prophet was an orphan when he was born, his father having died before his birth, and he lost his mother also when yet a boy. Therefore he enjoyed neither the tender caresses of a mother, nor the loving care of a father. Jesus Christ, on the other hand, was brought up by a righteous mother in all the sacred traditions of a nation in which prophets had appeared in abundance, and yet he did not attain to that eminence in the perfection of morals to which an

---

101. 2:47   102. 2:61   103. 57:19

orphan Arab attained without the help of any human being. Jesus had his teachers besides his father and mother to instruct him and to look after him, but the Holy Prophet Muḥammad, may peace and the blessings of God be upon him, had neither; and yet the treasures of wisdom met with in the Holy Qur'ān would be sought in vain in the Gospels. He was placed in these circumstances to show how the chastening effected by the Divine hand surpasses all chastening. Therefore the Prophet's being brought up as an orphan makes his greatness shine all the more brilliantly.

But if the Prophet's mother did not live to see and share the great transformation he brought about in Arabia, the Holy Qur'ān is not altogether silent with respect to her. Nay, it speaks not only of the parents of the Holy Prophet but of all his grandfathers and grandmothers as well. Thus it says:

> And rely on the Mighty, the Merciful, Who sees you when you stand up, and your turning among those Who prostrate themselves before Allāh.[104]

What is meant by *turning among those who prostrate*? Ibn 'Abbās says, it means "the turning from father to son in their loins until his mother brought him forth." This shows that the Prophet's parents and grand-parents were all among those who were obedient to God. This verse therefore not only speaks of the holiness of his parents but of his grand-parents as well, while according to the Bible this honour was certainly not attained by Jesus Christ, for of some of his grand-parents it does not speak well, though we do not give any credit to such statements and look upon them as alterations effected in the word of God.

---

104. 26:217-219

3. Extraordinary Occurences at the Time of Birth

The third argument in this connection deals with a very unimportant matter. I may, however, say a few words about it before taking up the next question. It is asserted that extraordinary occurences were noticed at the birth of Jesus and not at the birth of the Holy Prophet Muḥammad:

> Extraordinary happenings occurred at the birth of Christ, for instance, a withered palm-tree became green and gave fruit, a fountain flowed, angels came down to comfort Mary as is mentioned in the second section of the chapter Mary. But at the birth of Ḥaḍrat Muḥammad, no miracle or extraordinary happening occurred; and no proof of miracles is met with in the Qur'ān; therefore the son of Mary excels the son of Āminah.

It is a fact that the Holy Qur'ān does not speak of any miracle having taken place at the birth of Jesus. An angel no doubt comforted Mary, but that was due to her giving birth to the child under very awkward circumstances. It was in an inn, but there being no place inside she had to wrap him in "swaddling clothes" and lay him "in a manger." The Holy Qur'ān does not mention these details but from it too appears that Mary was at the time on a journey and did not enjoy the comforts of a home or of a helper. She stood in need of comfort indeed, and it is in fact to direct attention to her great distress at the time of birth that the Holy Qur'ān speaks of the comfort given her by the angel. As regards the withered tree becoming green and the fountain flowing, the Qur'ān nowhere says so. All that it says is:

> And the throes of childbirth compelled her to betake herself to the trunk of a palm-tree ... Then a voice called out to her from beneath her: Grieve not, surely your Lord has made a stream to flow beneath you, and shake towards you the trunk

of the palm-tree, it will drop on you ripe dates, so eat and drink and refresh the eye.[105]

These verses show that the palm-tree was there already and the voice only directed Mary's attention to the fact that she could get both food and water without going far in search of them, there being fresh ripe dates on the palm-tree to which she had betaken herself to seek relief from the throes of childbirth, and fresh water in a stream that flowed beneath her.

Even if we suppose that there was a miracle in providing food for a woman, it dwarfs into insignificance before the mighty sign that was shown at the birth of the Holy Prophet Muḥammad, on whom be peace. The Holy Qur'ān speaks of this in clear terms:

> Have you not considered how your Lord dealt with the possessors of the elephant? Did He not cause their war to end in confusion and send down to prey upon them birds in flocks casting them against hard stones; so He rendered them like straw eaten up.[106]

The reference here is to the memorable invasion of Makka by Abraha, the Christian viceroy at Yaman, of the king of Abyssinia. Abraha's object was to destroy the Ka'ba so as to divert the Arab religious enthusiasm, as well as the Arab trade, to Sana'ā where he had built a magnificent cathedral for the purpose. This army is known in Arabia as the *aṣḥāb al fīl*, or the possessors of the elephant, because of the presence of elephants in it. When the huge army was only some three days' march from Makka, 'Abdul-Muṭṭalib, the grandfather of the Holy Prophet, unable to defend the Ka'ba, thus prayed to God: "Defend, O Lord! Thine own House, and suffer not the cross to triumph over the Ka'ba." A virulent form of small-pox or some other pestilence broke out in Abraha's army which retreated in confusion and dismay and the Ka'ba was thus miraculously saved from the evil intentions of the Christians. And history shows that this happened in the year 570 of the Christian era, the year of the birth of our Holy Prophet. This is indeed a mighty sign which was shown to

---

105. 19:23-26   106. ch. 105

the world at the birth of our Holy Prophet. What significance can be attached to Mary's finding dates on a palm-tree and water in a stream when compared with the wonderful sign shown at the advent of the Holy Prophet! This is related in the Holy Qur'ān, while numerous other signs that took place at his birth are met with in the Reports.

Chapter 4

The Call

The next argument of the superiority of Jesus is even more interesting than the first three. We are told:

> Christ's speaking in cradle and being granted the book and the prophethood in infancy, is a very clear and conclusive argument of his excellence above all other prophets. As against this, Muhammad claimed to be the recipient of a book and prophethood at a time when passing youth he had attained to old age and there probably remained no deficiency in his worldly experience. Therefore Christ is superior to him.

Is there a child in the world that does not speak in the cradle? The answer is clear: none but a dumb child. And the Holy Qur'ān mentions Jesus speaking while a child in the cradle along with his speaking when of old age: "And he shall speak to the people when in the cradle and when of old age".[107] The same importance must be attached to both. If the words can be construed to mean that it shall be miraculous in him to speak in old age, then of course we are justified in taking the talk in the cradle also to be miraculous but not otherwise. It may, however, be asked that if it is such an ordinary circumstance, why it has been mentioned at all. There are two reasons for that. In the first place, to give comfort to Mary that he shall live to an old age, the cradle being mentioned simply as opposed to very old age. And there is a report from the Holy Prophet that Jesus Christ lived to the age of 120 years. And, secondly, and that is the more important purpose underlying the words, to show that he would pass through all the conditions of life through which

---

107. 3:45

every human child has to pass, from the unconscious *infant* in the cradle he will pass through all the natural stages to the condition of the hoary-headed man, to point out that he is nothing more than a mortal.

The second point is Christ's being granted the book and prophethood in infancy. Great stress is laid upon this point as proving the undoubted superiority of Jesus Christ to the Holy Prophet Muhammad, may peace and the blessings of God be upon him, who was granted prophethood when he had passed youth and had reached almost an old age. It is even hinted that the claim to prophethood in an advanced age is the result of worldly experience and not due to the inner call which proceeds from a Divine source. Now this is the most regrettable aspect of the Christian controversy. Objections are advanced against Islām so unscrupulously that not the least respect is shown to the doctrines even of the Christian religion. When was Abraham called to prophethood? When did Moses and Aaron receive the Divine message? Was there not the same worldly experience in their case? Nay, one may ask, when did Christ himself receive the Divine message according to the sacred Scriptures of the Christians? What was the age of Jesus when he was baptised by John the Baptist? How old was he when "the heavens were opened unto him and he saw the spirit of God descending like a dove and lighting upon him"? Did it happen in his infancy, or when he had attained the advanced age of thirty years? If the Gospels tell us that he was called at thirty years, is it befitting for a Christian to distort the words of the Qur'ān to make Jesus receive the message when not yet quite a day old and then to call this as the proof of his superiority to the Holy Prophet Muhammad, because he received the message at forty? Such weapons should be left for those who aim at the meaner advantages of this life, but their true use in the hands of a religious man whose object is to preach virtue does not speak well of him.

Let us see now what the Holy Qur'ān says. After speaking of the birth of Jesus Christ, the Holy Qur'ān goes on to say:

> He (i.e. Jesus) said: surely I am a servant of Allāh. He has given me the book and made me a prophet. And He has

made me blessed wherever I may be, and He has enjoined on me prayer and poor-rate so long as I live.[108]

The words of these verses are so clearly the words of a man of advanced age that there does not exist the slightest justification for ascribing them to an infant: "He has given me the book and made me a prophet." Supposing that prophethood could be given in some inexplicable manner to an infant not a day old yet, how could the book be given to him? The giving of the book means that there are certain teachings which he inculcates. How could an infant a day old say that he had been teaching his doctrines to the people. This would mean that he had been teaching even before he came into existence. We cannot put upon the words of the Holy Qur'ān an interpretation which is rejected by the merest common sense. The words that follow, however, make still more ludicrous the supposition that a new-born infant was speaking: "He has enjoined on me prayer and poor-rate so long as I live." This shows that the injunction to pray and pay the poor-rate had already been given. Did Jesus obey that injunction which he was to carry out *so long as he lived*? No human brain can entertain the conception that an infant born only twelve hours before could carry out the injunction to say prayers, and more than that, to pay the poor-rate. Poor-rate on what? On the "swaddling clothes" in which he was wrapped up at his birth? He had no other property on which he could pay the poor-rate, and it is doubtful even if the cloth in which he was wrapped up, so that he might not move his limbs freely, could be called his property on which he should pay the poor-rate.

The case is too clear to need further comment. The words could not be the words of a new-born infant. These are the words of a man who has received the book containing the doctrines which he has been teaching, who has been going about from one place to another — "wherever I go" — who says his prayers regularly, and who has got his own property on which he pays the poor-rate. The words were therefore spoken after Jesus began teaching his doctrines to the

---

108. 19:30-31

people. The one argument that is given in support of the other conclusion is that the previous verses speak of the birth of childhood of Jesus. If the words of the verses under discussion could possibly bear the interpretation that they were uttered by a new-born infant, the evidence of the context could be brought forth to support that interpretation. But what the words cannot bear, even the context cannot make them bear. And it should be borne in mind that in the case of the histories of the former prophets narrated in the Holy Qur'ān, the context cannot help us much, for the Holy Qur'ān does not relate the whole story from beginning to end, but often omits long portions, taking up only the particular incidents which serve the purpose for which the story is related.

Take as an example the story of John the Baptist which is related immediately before the story of Jesus. There Zacharias prays for a son, and he receives the good news that a son will be born to him. "How shall I have a son and my wife is barren?" The answer is:

> So shall it be ... I created you before when you were nothing." He asks for a sign and is told not to speak to people for three days. The order is obeyed: "So he went forth to his people from his place of worship, then he made known to them that they should glorify Allāh morning and evening. O John! take hold of the book with strength, and We granted him wisdom while yet a child".[109]

If the reasoning followed in the story of Jesus were to be followed here, the conclusion would be inevitable that even the three days of Zacharias' silence had not yet passed when John the Baptist was there with a book. But we cannot be justified in drawing this conclusion for we know that all that should happen in the natural course before he should receive a book must have happened, and the Holy Qur'ān has only left out the mention of that. Similarly, it is in the case of Jesus, with this difference that his being conceived by Mary and his birth are also mentioned, and this account is followed by a brief reference to his ministry, the intermediate incidents being

---

109. 19:11-12

left out as in the case of John. There is not the slightest evidence in the Holy Qur'ān that the ordinary laws of nature were relaxed in the case of Jesus.

According to the Holy Qur'ān, forty years is the age of the moral completion of man: "Until when he attains his maturity and reaches forty years".[110] All prophets are raised at the age of forty, and a mistake seems to have been made by the Christians in the case of Jesus who is said to have been thirty years old when he received the call. Thus there is no difference on the score of age between the prophets of God and even supposing that one prophet was called at the age of thirty and another at the age of forty, this difference does not show the superiority of one or the inferiority of the other.

What shows the greatness of the Holy Prophet Muḥammad, however, is that the first forty years of his life were so well spent that they stand as an everlasting testimony to his truth, a circumstance lacking in the case of all other prophets including Jesus Christ. So deeply rooted was the welfare of humanity in the Prophet's heart that even before he received the great Divine call, he spent the best hours of his life in giving relief to the poor. It was for this reason that his most intimate companion, his wife Khadījah, made the following remarks on receiving the news of the Divine call:

> By no means! Allāh will not bring you to disgrace, for you do keep the ties of kinship, and you do bear the burden of the weak, and you do earn for those who are penniless, and you do honour the guest, and you do help those actually in distress.[111]

Could anybody conceive a nobler object of life than that? And yet this was before he was raised to the dignity of prophethood. The forty years of his life were thus spent, not in *worldly experience*, but in giving help to the poor, the weak and the distressed. Nobody could make the same claim for Jesus or any other prophet. The Holy Prophet's life was one devoted to the service of humanity from his very childhood to the last moment, and if he was called at forty, he

---

110. 46:15   111. *Bukhārī*

had been doing the greatest work of a prophet long before that. Thus among all the reformers of the world, Muḥammad, may peace and the blessings of God be upon him, occupies the highest position because not a minute of his life was spent for any object other than the service of humanity, and he was a prophet in fact from his childhood though he did not receive the call until the age of forty.

Another circumstance which singles him out among the prophets of the world is the fact that his righteousness was so great and perfect, before he was called to the office of prophet, that not only he did not stand in need of being baptised by somebody as Jesus did, but what is much more, the whole nation was so fully convinced of his great and wonderful virtues, so deeply conscious of his truthfulness and righteousness, that it had given him the title of *al-Amīn*, or *the righteous one*. This recognition by a stubborn people like the Arabs bespeaks a degree of righteousness in a man which surpasses every conception of righteousness and this honour is not shared by any other prophet with him. Thus the first forty years of his life were not only spent in the service of humanity, but at the same time they afford an evidence of the perfection of his righteousness. It is to this that the Holy Qur'ān calls attention in the words:

> Indeed I have lived a lifetime among you before it: do you not then understand.[112]

---

112. 10:16

Chapter 5

Circumstances Relating to Death

1. The Alleged Ascent to Heaven

Another argument of Christ's superiority runs thus:

> From the Qur'ān it is manifest that when the enemies wished to seize Christ, angels came down from heaven and took him up with this body of clay to heaven and thus God guarded him from wretched unbelievers. But when the enemies surrounded Muḥammad in Mecca, neither there came an angel to save him, nor was he taken up to heaven; but like ordinary men walked down through a thorny desert, hidden from the enemy's sight, to take shelter in a dark cave, then flying from there took refuge with the Helpers at Medina. Is it not a difference of heaven and earth? ... These facts make it clear that Christ is superior to Muḥammad.

It appears from the above quotation that the writer is either quite ignorant of the Holy Qur'ān, or intentionally misrepresents the Holy Book as to the supposed ascent of Jesus to heaven. That the latter is the case is more probable, for while he claims that it is manifest from the Qur'ān, he does not quote a single verse; such quotations are abundantly given where they could be found. It is a fact that there is not a single verse in the Holy Qur'ān stating that when Christ was about to be arrested angels came down from heaven and that he was

taken up to heaven with this body of clay. While there is not even the
remotest hint to the coming down of angels which is merely a pious
invention, even Christ's going up to heaven with this body of clay,
notwithstanding what the majority of the Muslims believe, is
nowhere mentioned in the Holy Qur'ān.

What is wonderful, however, is not that the Holy Qur'ān does
not speak of Jesus' rising to heaven with this body of clay, but that
even the Gospels fail to furnish the necessary testimony. If such an
incident really took place, it was the most important event of the life
of Christ and it ought to have been not only recorded unanimously
by all the Gospel-writers but should further have been shown to have
taken place in the presence of large crowds of men, for a miracle
loses all its value if it is not performed publicly. But what have we
got? Matthew is quite silent as to Jesus' rising to heaven. St. John is
also silent. Two of the four Gospels do not know anything about the
supposed ascent to heaven. This omission casts very serious doubt on
the truth of the allegation of ascent to heaven; for if it took place, it
was the most important event of Jesus' life, more important than a
thousand miracles of healing the sick, far more important than the
crucifixion itself and the post-crucifixion appearances, and no Gospel
writer could omit it.

What have the other two Gospels to say? Luke says:

> And it came to pass, while he blessed them, he was parted
> from them, and carried up into heaven.[113]

A strange miracle this! Not a single Jew was there to witness the
scene. Not even all the believers were present. Jesus was carried up
into heaven stealthily lest the Jews getting information about it
should frustrate the attempt! If there really was an ascent, how was
it that not a single person except the eleven saw it? The whole of
Jerusalem could have easily witnessed it and people would all have
become believers immediately. The matter, on the other hand, was
kept secret, and great was the secrecy that not even the believers got
any news of it. Does it not show clearly that the parting was brought

---

113. Luke 24:51

about not by Jesus going up into heaven, but by some other manner which it was necessary to conceal. It was clearly a *flight* which was to be kept secret, for if the slightest news of it had got out, the life of Jesus would have been in great danger. And thus Jesus, according to the events narrated in the Gospels, fled secretly, *hidden from the enemy's sight*, to use the very words of the slighters of the Prophet's flight. That this is the only right conclusion of what is narrated by Luke in his last chapter is established conclusively by the fact that the words *and carried up into heaven* are really a later interpolation, for we are told by J.R. Dummelow in his commentary on the Bible that "a few ancient authorities omit these words." Thus if two of the Gospels entirely discredit the story of the Ascension and do not give it a place in their record of the life of Jesus, the words of the third, which are looked upon as the basis of the theory, are not merely out of place in the narration of events, but are actually not met with in ancient manuscripts.

Three of the Gospels being thus against the ascent to heaven, the fourth need not detain us long. The story as related in Mark is still more incredible. In the concluding chapter of this Gospel we find that the women who went early to the sepulchre were told by a young man clad in white, apparently none other than Jesus himself, to "tell his disciples and Peter that he goeth before you into Galilee"[114], while the 19th verse of the same chapter gives the unexpected news that "he was received up into heaven and sat on the right hand of God." In the first place, the writer of this passage describes his being "received up into heaven" and sitting "on the right hand of God" as two incidents of which he was an eyewitness. The words of Luke "carried up" are safer, because they indicate that the narrator only saw him being carried up. But the narrator in Mark seems to have gone up to heaven along with Jesus, where he saw that Jesus "was received up into heaven and sat on the right hand of God." Who can think of relying on such testimony, and accepting on its basis such an extraordinary thing as the rising of a man to heaven? Secondly, the 19th verse clearly contradicts the 7th verse of the same chapter. The

---

114. Mark 16:17

7th verse tells us that Jesus intended to go to Galilee; the 19th tells us that he went up to heaven. Apparently the two statements are inconsistent with each other.

But what is more, the concluding twelve verses of Mark are shown by recent investigation to be an interpolation, and thus it is proved beyond all doubt that the 19th verse of Mark which states that Jesus "was received up into heaven" must be rejected altogether, and the last testimony to the ascent of Jesus to heaven thus vanishes into nothingness. The last twelve verses of the sixteenth chapter of Mark are admittedly not by St. Mark. Thus says Dummelow, the commentator of the Bible:

> Internal evidence points definitely to the conclusion that the last twelve verses are not by St. Mark. For (1) the true conclusion certainly contained a Galilean appearance[115], and this does not. (2) The style is that of a bare catalogue of facts, and quite unlike St. Mark's usual wealth of graphic detail. (3) The section contains numerous words and expressions never used by St. Mark. (4) Mark 16:9 makes an abrupt fresh start, and is not continuous with the preceding narrative. (5) Mary Magdalene is spoken of[116] as if she had not been mentioned before, although she has just been alluded to twice.[117]

This settles the matter conclusively. The last twelve verses of Mark are not a part of the original manuscript, and one uncial manuscript gives quite a different termination. Instead of the last twelve verses we have there:

> And they reported all the things that had been commanded them briefly (or immediately) to the companions of Peter. And after this Jesus himself also sent forth by them from the east even unto the west the holy and incorruptible preaching of eternal salvation.

---

115. Mark 16:7, cp. 14:28   116. 16:9   117. 15:47; 16:1

How did these twelve verses find a place here? The account is interesting as given by the same commentator:

> The Gospel of St. Mark, being the first extensive and authoritative account of our Lord's life, as distinguished from His discourses, attained at its first publication (A.D. 55-60) a considerable circulation first in the west and afterwards in the east. At the time it concluded with an account of the Galilean appearance, which is now only to be found in St. Matthew[118]. The subsequent publication of the first and third Gospels, which incorporated practically its whole subject-matter, and were far more interesting as containing discourses, practically drove it out of circulation. When at the close of the Apostolic age an attempt was made (probably in Rome) to collect the authentic memorials of the Apostles and their companions, a copy of the neglected second Gospel was not easily found. The one that was actually discovered, and was used to multiply copies, had lost its last leaf, and so a fitting termination (the present appendix) was added by another hand. A recently discovered Armenian MS. (1891) definitely ascribes the appendix to Ariston, i.e. probably Aristion, "a disciple of the Lord mentioned by Papias (A.D. 130)".

Indeed if the early Christian Fathers had not been so adept in the art of making up deficiencies in spoiled manuscripts, a very large portion of the present Gospels would never have reached us. Thus not only two Gospels, but really all the four canonical Gospels, know nothing about Jesus' ascent to heaven and the theory is evidently of much later growth, when evidence was fabricated in the form of interpolations in two of the Gospels.

On the other hand, the Bible records Elijah's ascent to heaven, and he must therefore be regarded as much superior to Jesus Christ from a Christian's point of view. "And Elijah went up by a whirlwind into heaven".[119] Elijah's ascent to heaven is so clear that

---

118. 28:16   119. 2 Kings 2:11

according to the Bible record it was witnessed by another prophet Elisha who even "took the mantle of Elijah that fell from him." Another parallel is that of Enoch who "walked with God and he was not; for God took him".[120] This was indeed the material on which was built up the theory of Jesus' ascension by Christian zealots who were eager to ascribe to their hero whatever greatness they met with in others.

Does the Holy Qur'ān support the theory of Jesus' bodily ascent to heaven? Not in the least. Not once does the Holy Book say that Jesus was taken up *to heaven*. It speaks of his *rafa'* to Allāh, i.e. exaltation in the presence of God, but never of his ascent with the body, and never mentions the *heaven* in connection with his *rafa'* which has wrongly been supposed to mean *ascent*. The Holy Qur'ān speaks of the *rafa'* of Jesus on two occasions. In the third chapter we have: "O Jesus! I will cause you to die and exalt you in My presence".[121] And in the fourth: "And they killed him not for sure; nay, Allāh exalted him in His presence".[122] In both places I have rendered the word *rafa'* as meaning *exaltation*, as the great commentator Rāzī himself says when commenting on 3:54, *"Rafa'* here is *the exalting in degree and in praise not in place and direction."* There exists some misunderstanding as to the meaning of the word *rafa'* which means both the *raising* of a thing and the *exaltation* of a person (see Lane, *Arabic-English Lexicon*). The latter is always the significance when the *rafa'* of a person by God is spoken of and the clearest testimony on this point is afforded by the word *al-Rāfi'* which is one of the names of God. All Arabic lexicons agree that *al-Rāfi'* means "the Exalter of the believer by prospering him and of his saints by teaching them" (Lane, *Arabic-English Lexicon*). Therefore when Allāh is spoken of as granting *rafa'* to a person, the *only* significance that the words convey is that He has granted him *exaltation*, and not that He has raised him up bodily from a lower level to a higher one.

---

120. Gen. 5:24   121. 3:54   122. 4:157-158

The Holy Qur'ān and the sayings of the Holy Prophet are full of examples of the true meaning of the word, while not a single example is to be met with in the whole Arabic literature in which the *rafaʿ* of a man by God means raising him up bodily. Thus we have in 43:32, "And We have exalted some of them above others in degrees" where in the original we have *rafaʿnā*. Again in 6:84 and 12:76, "We exalt in dignity whom We please." These are general statements showing that the *rafaʿ* of a person by God means his *exaltation in rank*, and not raising him up in body. Indeed if the latter significance were acceptable under any circumstances, the Divine law should have been that the righteous should all have been translated bodily from the earth to some higher region.

Two concrete examples may also be cited. The Holy Qur'ān 7:176 thus speaks of a person who rejects the truth after it has been brought to him:

> And if We had pleased We would certainly have *exalted* him thereby, but he clung to the earth and followed his low desire.

All the commentators agree in explaining *rafaʿ* in the above verse as meaning *exaltation*. Thus the *Fatḥ al-Bayān* explains the meaning as "exalting to the place of the learned," or "exalting so as to make him enter enter paradise." *Baiḍāwī* accepts a similar interpretation, i.e., "exaltation to the place of the righteous." *Ibn Jarīr*, explaining the word *rafaʿ*, used in this verse says:

> And *rafaʿ* conveys a number of significances; among these is the exaltation in rank in the Divine presence, and the exaltation in the greatness and excellences of the world and the exaltation in good renown.

All this shows that the *rafaʿ* of a person by God in the language of the Holy Qur'ān means nothing but *exaltation*.

The other example is that of Enoch. Speaking of him the Holy Qur'ān says: "And mention Idrīs in the Book; surely he was a truthful man, a prophet; and We exalted him to an elevated state".[123] In this case, the same misunderstanding has arisen to a certain degree as that in the case of Jesus Christ, and the reason of it is to be met with in what the Bible says of that prophet. Gen. 5:24, on this point has already been quoted and though the words there are not very clear as regards his being taken up alive to heaven, but even the New Testament writers were influenced by the prevailing Jewish belief, for in Heb. 11:5, we have:

> By faith Enoch was translated that he should not see death and was not found because God had translated him.

Some commentators of the Holy Qur'ān were also influenced by the same idea, and accordingly they interpreted the above words as meaning Enoch's being taken up alive to heaven. But the more learned among them have plainly ascribed these ideas to the influence of the Israelite story-tellers. Thus *Ibn Kathīr* says of the stories of Enoch's being taken up alive to heaven as met with in some commentaries: "These are among the Israelite stories of Ka'b and some of these are unacceptable." The *Fath al-Bayān* gives a similar judgement: "These are the Israelite stories which Ka'b used to narrate." The *Ruh al-Ma'ānī* gives the significance of *rafa'* here as *exaltation to "the great dignity of prophethood and nearness."* Hasan explains it as meaning *exaltation to paradise.* The *Rūh al-Ma'ānī* which I have already quoted concludes its discussion of this point in the following words: "And this *rafa'* must be in respect of the greatness of rank and the exaltation of dignity, for that is a praiseworthy thing, and the merely being uplifted to a higher place is nothing."

The misunderstanding in the case of Enoch very clearly explains how the misunderstanding arose in the case of Jesus Christ, and anyone who considers the matter critically in the latter case can as easily get out of the error as the more critical commentators have got out of the misunderstanding with respect to Enoch. Certain prevailing Jewish or Christian stories influenced the ideas of some commentators and they misinterpreted the word *rafa'*. In fact, the use

---

123. 19:56-57

of the word, not only in the Holy Qur'ān but also in the sayings of the Holy Prophet and the whole of Islamic literature, settles the meaning conclusively. For instance, every Muslim is taught to pray while sitting between the two prostrations in his prayer: "O Allāh grant me protection and have mercy on me and guide me and grant me sustenance and exalt me ..." Now this prayer for *rafa'*, or exaltation, by every Muslim would be a meaningless prayer if it were supposed that God's granting *rafa'* to a man meant his bodily translation to some upper region; for from the great Prophet down to this day, not the prayer of a single Muslim has been accepted in this sense. Again, there are many sayings of the Holy Prophet regarding humbleness in which the word *rafa'* is used always indicating exaltation of degrees: "Whoever humbles himself for God's sake, God exalts him"; and in one report we have the words: "Whoever makes himself humble for God's sake, God *exalts* him to the seventh heaven by means of a chain," the word in the original being *rafa'* in both the cases. Notwithstanding such express words apparently indicating a bodily translation, no one has ever supposed that the meek and the humble are ever raised in body to the seventh heaven.

The above examples are sufficient to establish the fact conclusively that by the *rafa'* of Jesus Christ is meant *his exaltation in rank and degree and not his bodily translation*. And this is in fact clear from the very words used about him: "I will cause you to die and exalt you in My presence", where the exaltation follows death, and could therefore only be exaltation in rank. In the other verse: "And they killed him not for sure; nay, Allāh exalted him in His presence", the exaltation is brought in as a contrast with killing on the cross; for death on the cross was looked upon as subjecting a man to abasement, such a person being held to have been accursed and driven out of Divine presence. Thus Paul says:

> Christ has redeemed us from the curse of the law, being made a curse for us: for it is written, cursed is every one that hangeth on a tree".[124]

---

124. Gal. 3:13

It is to denounce the false belief of Jesus Christ being under the curse of God that the Holy Qur'ān speaks of his *rafa'* or exaltation.

As regards the manner in which our Holy Prophet was saved from the hands of his enemies, the chief point that distinguishes him from Jesus Christ is that he never fell into their hands to be treated in the humiliating manner in which Jesus was treated, who, though saved from an accursed death on the cross, fell yet so completely into the enemy's hands that he was made to resemble a man who had actually met death on the cross. But the Holy Prophet, notwithstanding that he fled alone through a host of enemies that had surrounded his house to put him to death, never met with the humiliation which it had been the fate of Jesus Christ to meet. Though alone, yet so well did the angels guard him that not one of the hosts assembled around his house could see him while he passed through them. Even in the numerous battles that he had to fight, though many a time he was left alone among enemies who thirsted for his blood, yet never was he actually overpowered by them. He no doubt received wounds in one battle, but the enemy could not lay their hands on him, and Divine protection was always with him to a far greater degree than it was with Jesus Christ.

2. The Death of Christ

We will now take the next argument of Christ's superiority:

It is one of the admissions made by Islām that Christ is alive up to this time in the heavens with this body of clay, and that notwithstanding a mortal body he is free from the needs of a mortal, i.e. does not stand in need of eating and drinking, and in spite of being a mortal he fulfils the (Divine) attribute of being now as he ever was. As against this, it is written thus of the children of Adam in the Qur'ān: "Therein shall you live and therein shall you die and from it shall you be raised." And elsewhere: "Have We not made the earth to draw together to itself the living and the dead?" Again it is written of all the prophets: "And We did not make them bodies not eating the food and they were not to abide," i.e. We have not made for them such bodies that they should be able to live for ever without eating and drinking. Therefore one who can live without eating and drinking notwithstanding a mortal body is unique and superior to all the other prophets, otherwise this Qur'ānic verse shall have to be admitted as being wrong. Christ who from about two thousand years is alive in the heavens without food and drink cannot be counted as one of the apostles and the prophets whose life depends on eating and drinking. If then Muḥammad does not possess these attributes, is it not manifest that Christ is superior to and by far greater than he?

If Christ's bodily ascent to heaven turns out to be only a pious fabrication of the Christians innocently taken up as a fact by some Muslim commentators, his being alive in heaven meets the same fate. As regards the Qur'ān, it has been made clear already that it nowhere speaks of a bodily ascent; it only speaks of his spiritual exaltation. The writer quoted above is aware of the fact that the Holy Qur'ān does not contain the slightest evidence of Jesus' being alive in the heavens, and therefore he takes shelter in the so-called *admissions of Islām*. Now to call that an admission of Islām which is believed by one portion of the Muslim world, even if the belief is held by a majority, is a grave misrepresentation. Nothing can be said to have been admitted by Islām that is not admitted in the Holy Qur'ān or trustworthy sayings of the Holy Prophet. But it is a fact that both the Holy Qur'ān and the collections of Reports do not contain a single word as to Jesus' being *alive in the heavens*, and among the Muslims there have always been men who have held that Jesus Christ was dead. The name of Mālik, one of the four great Imāms recognised by the *Ahl al-Sunnat*, may be mentioned here. The *Majma' al-Bihār*, a dictionary of Reports, says in plain words when discussing the meaning of the word *ḥakam*: "And Mālik says that he (i.e. Jesus Christ) died". Similarly *Ikmāl al-Mu'lam*, a commentary of the *Ṣaḥīḥ Muslim*, admits that it is written in the *'Utabiyyah* that Mālik believed in the death of Jesus Christ.

I have said that the Holy Qur'ān does not contain a single word showing that Christ is alive in the heavens. On the other hand, it plainly speaks of his death. The following verses can bear no other significance:

> And when Allāh will say: O Jesus, son of Mary! did you say to men, Take me and my mother for two gods besides Allāh, he will say, Glory be to Thee, it did not befit me that I should say what I had no right to say ... I did not say to them aught save what Thou didst enjoin me with, That serve Allāh, my Lord and your Lord; and I was witness of them so long as I was among them, but when Thou didst cause me to die, Thou wert the Watcher over them, and Thou art witness of all things.[125]

These words afford a conclusive testimony that the teachings of Jesus Christ were not corrupted until after his death — the words *when Thou didst cause me to die* being too clear to allow any other interpretation. The word *tawaffā* which is used here carries the significance of *causing death*, and this is also the interpretation of Ibn 'Abbās as noted in the *Bukhārī*. There is no room for the slightest doubt here, while further light is thrown on this point by a report recorded in the *Bukhārī*, according to which the Holy Prophet used concerning himself the very words which are here put into the mouth of Jesus. He is reported to have said (see chapter on the commentary of *āl-'Imrān*) that he would be shown on the Day of Resurrection certain men who had gone against his teachings, and that he would thereon say:

> What the righteous servant (i.e. Jesus) said, I was witness of them so long as I was among them, but when Thou didst cause me to die, Thou wert the Watcher over them.

This report is another conclusive testimony that it was in the one case after the death of Jesus, and in the other after that of the Holy Prophet, that their respective followers went against their teachings.

---

125. 5:116-117

This is also in accordance with what the Gospel says: "While I was with them in the world, I kept them in Thy name".[126]

There are other reports also plainly speaking of the death of Jesus Christ. According to one of these, the Holy Prophet is reported to have said: "Had Moses and Jesus been alive, nought would have availed them but that they should follow me." According to another still we are told that "Jesus lived for one hundred and twenty years." With such clear testimony before us, it is a mistake to hold that the Holy Qur'ān and the sayings of the Holy Prophet speak of Jesus as being alive in the heavens, on the basis simply of the prophecy relating to his re-appearance which must be interpreted in the same manner as the prophecy of the re-appearance of Elijah was interpreted by no less an authority than Jesus Christ, viz. that it necessitates the appearance, not of the person named, but of somebody else who should appear in his spirit and power, but more of this later on.

If any inference as to Jesus' being alive is drawn from the words, "And they did not kill him, nor did they put him to death on the cross",[127] it can only be drawn in defiance of logic. If it is related of a person who lived two thousand years ago that he was not killed or that he did not meet with his death on the cross, is there a sane person in this world who would draw from this the conclusion that he is still alive? But it may be asked, what does the Holy Qur'ān then say as to what happened to him? The answer to this has already been given; the Holy book states in the clearest possible words that God caused him to die a natural death. And here after negativing Jesus' death on the cross or by killing, it goes on to say, "But the matter was made dubious to them," or the same words may be interpreted as meaning, "But he was made to resemble (one dying on the cross) to them." Both interpretations carry the same significance, viz. that his enemies thought they had put him to death on the cross while he was actually left alive. And when we go to the Gospels we find ample testimony of the truth of this assertion.

---

126. John 17:12   127. 4:157

It appears from the Gospels that Jesus escaped with his life from the cross, and though he was treated as a dead man, yet there were circumstances which even then made the people doubt his death. It has never been seriously contended that Jesus remained on the cross for a very short time, so short indeed that it was impossible that the tardy method of putting to death by crucifixion should kill a man within such a short interval. As further proof of this we find that the two men crucified along with Jesus were still alive when taken down. Secondly, the breaking of legs was resorted to in the case of the other two but was dispensed with in the case of Jesus.[128] Thirdly, the side of Jesus being pierced, blood rushed out which was a sure sign of life.[129] Fourthly, when Pilate was told that Jesus had died, he did not believe.[130] Fifthly, Jesus was not buried like the ordinary culprits but was given into the charge of a wealthy disciple[131] who put him into a spacious room hewn into the side of a rock, a stone being rolled against the door.[132] Sixthly, when the tomb was visited on the third day, the stone was found to have been removed from its mouth.[133] This was clearly done to enable Jesus to walk out of his resting-place when he had recovered on the third day. Seventhly, Jesus disguised himself as a gardener after he had recovered, as is shown by the fact that Mary when she saw him believed him to be the gardener.[134] Such disguise would not have been needed, if Jesus had risen from the dead. Eighthly, it was in the same body of flesh that the disciples saw Jesus,[135] and the wounds were still deep enough for a man to thrust his hand in.[136] Ninthly, he still felt hunger and ate as his disciples ate.[137] Tenthly, in all post-crucifixion appearances Jesus is found concealing and hiding himself for he feared being discovered.[138]

All these facts point conclusively to the truth of the statement made in the Holy Qur'ān that Jesus was not killed, nor did he die on the cross, but was likened to one dead and thus escaped with his life, afterwards dying a natural death, as is affirmed by the Holy Qur'ān.

---

128. John 19:31-33 129. John 19:34   130. Mark 15:44   131. John 19:38
132. John 19:41; 20:1   133. John 20:1   134. John 20:15
135. Luke 24:39   136. John 20:27   137. Luke 24:39-43 138. John 20:19

As to the second statement that other prophets ate food and that Jesus possesses a unique mortal body inasmuch as he does not stand in need of food, it is also devoid of truth. In fact, when it is shown that Jesus died a natural death, all assertions based on the supposition of his being alive fall to the ground. It is, however, a noteworthy fact that both the Gospels and the Holy Qur'ān speak of Jesus as standing in need of food like ordinary mortals. In the Gospels there are many incidents showing how Jesus felt hunger. In the first place, "when he had fasted for forty days and forty nights, he was afterward an hungered".[139] With such a clear statement in the Gospels, it is a foolish attempt to sit down to prove that Jesus possessed a unique body which did not stand in need of food. Another incident shows rather the darker side of this human frailty:

> And on the morrow, when they were come from Bethany, he was hungry: and seeing a fig tree afar off having leaves, he came, if haply he might find anything thereon: and when he came to it, he found nothing but leaves; for the time of figs was not *yet*. And Jesus answered and said unto it, No man eat fruit of thee hereafter for ever.[140]

To curse a tree for not giving fruit when it was not the time for it to give fruit yet, is the most strange thing that a sensible person can do. And if in response to that curse God too proved so partial to Jesus that he made the fig-tree to wither away presently, that is still more strange. Can this action of Jesus Christ be distinguished, if the Gospel record is to be believed true, from the action of a man who blinded by anger ascribes his own fault to another and forthwith curses him? Was it not Jesus' own fault that, pinched by hunger, he ran to a tree to find figs on it while it was not the time of figs. J.R. Dummelow says commenting on this incident that "Jesus was not really hungry or expected to find figs". A strange comment in the face of the clear words in the Gospels that *he was hungry* and that he came to the tree that *haply he might find anything thereon*! And then we are told that this miracle of wrath was wrought on a tree and not

---

139. Matt. 4:2   140. Mark 11:12-14

upon a man to give proof of his great love for man. But the question is, what testimony does the incident afford as to Jesus himself being so overcome by hunger as not to know what the Gospel-writer knew, that it was not the time of figs yet, and then being so overcome by anger that he cursed a tree for not bearing fruit out of season. What would we think of a man living in the Punjab or Northern India running to a mango-tree in mid-winter or in the spring season and then cursing the mango-tree for not having ripe mangoes on it?

There are other instances showing how Jesus felt hungry at times. Even when risen from the dead, according to Christian belief, he stood in need of food. "Have you any meat?" was his first query when he met the apostles. "And they gave him a piece of a broiled fish, and of an honeycomb And he took it, and did eat before them".[141] If the Gospels then show Jesus as standing in need of food even after rising from among the dead, it is sheer folly to turn over the leaves of the Holy Qur'ān to make out a case for Jesus living without food. If, however, we turn to the Holy Qur'ān, we find it not only including Jesus among the mortal prophets when it says: "And We did not make them bodies not eating the food and they were not to abide," but going further and making the same statement about Jesus Christ in particular. Thus it says: "The Messiah, son of Mary, is but an Apostle; apostles before him have indeed passed away; and his mother was a truthful woman; they both used to eat food".[142] Why should Jesus be specially mentioned as possessing a mortal body which could not live without food when a general statement had already been made? My answer is: to leave no ground for those who should try to make Jesus an exception. But what is more, Jesus' eating food is mentioned here as an argument of his passing away like other apostles. The Messiah is only an apostle and apostles before him have passed away; hence he too must pass away and die like other mortal apostles; and to make the argument conclusive, it is added that both he and his mother ate food, because one who eats food cannot abide for ever, but must grow to a certain limit after which decline takes the place of growth. The momentary

141. Luke 24:42-43 142. 5:75

change that is taking place in the human body, the loss to which the mortal body is subject, requires food, and therefore the statement that Jesus required food is a conclusive argument that he suffered death.

This is also the reason why the Holy Qur'ān mentions Jesus' speaking in the cradle and old age. It is merely to point out that he possessed a body in no way differing from the ordinary mortal body. His first state is that of a baby in the cradle, and following the law of growth he attains to the prime of manhood, then he begins to decline and the signs of decrepitude appear in the hoary head of old age which must of necessity be followed by death.

Chapter 6

The Second Advent

The second advent of Jesus is considered to be another proof of Christ's greatness as compared with the Holy Prophet Muḥammad, may peace and the blessings of God be upon him, and the matter is argued thus:

> It is admitted by the Muslims that some time before the Day of Judgement, the Antichrist, the greatest seducer and the spreader of unbelief and irreligion, will make appearance, and to destroy him and to bring back the corrupt followers of Muḥammad to the right way and to establish the right religion, the Messiah will descend from the heaven ... If, therefore, Muḥammad was the Prophet of the last ages and the last of the prophets, why was it not destined that he should rise from his grave and remove this last tribulation? Why was it that the promised Messiah was entrusted with the work of the final overthrow of irreligion and corruption?

It is a grave misunderstanding that the Holy Qur'ān speaks anywhere of the return to life of Jesus Christ. That Jesus Christ will come after the Holy Prophet is just the reverse of what the Holy Qur'ān says:

> And when Jesus, son of Mary said, O children of Israel! surely I am the apostle of Allāh to you, verifying that which is before me of the Torah and giving the good news of an Apostle who will come after me, his name being Aḥmad".[143]

---

143. 61:6

This is a very clear statement, and it is rather strange that in spite of the express words that the Holy Prophet will come *after* Jesus, it is thought that Jesus must come after the Holy Prophet.

Again, as regards the successors of the Holy Prophet, the Holy Qur'ān is very clear:

> Allāh has promised to those of you who believe and do good that He will most certainly make them successors in the earth as He made successors those before them".[144]

The promise is given here in the plainest words that successors will be raised to the Holy Prophet from among the Muslims, and the coming of an Israelite prophet as a successor to the Holy Prophet is clearly against this. Jesus Christ cannot therefore be one of the successors of the Holy Prophet.

Another very clear testimony against the advent of Jesus Christ as a reformer among the Muslims is that he is plainly stated to be "an apostle to the children of Israel".[145] If he were destined to be also an apostle to the Muslims, the Holy Qur'ān would have added words to that effect. His description merely as an apostle to the Israelites is also conclusive testimony against the idea of Jesus' coming back to this world.

The clearest testimony on this point is however furnished by the following verse of the Holy Qur'ān: "He it is Who raised among the illiterates an Apostle from among themselves, who recites to them His messages and purifies them and teaches them the Book and the wisdom, although they were before certainly in clear error, and others from among them who have not yet joined them".[146] These verses make it clear that the Holy Prophet was not only the purifier and teacher of the Arabs, of his companions among whom he made his appearance, but also the purifier and teacher for ever of the whole Muslim world, of those who came after the companions, those who had not *yet joined* the companions. But as he could not live for ever, his purifying power and his office of teacher were transmitted to his

---

144. 24:55   145. 3:48   146. 62:2-3

companions who taught the next generation, and that generation again became the purifier and teacher of the one following it, the process continuing to the Day of Judgement. This verse thus does not leave any room at all for an Israelite prophet to become the purifier and teacher of the Muslim people. Least of all can it afford room to Jesus Christ, of whom we are plainly told that God himself did "teach him the book and the wisdom and the Torah and the Gospel".[147] The Holy Prophet Muhammad therefore cannot be the purifier and teacher of Jesus Christ, for as the Holy Qur'ān says, being a prophet, he was taught and purified directly by God. If he therefore comes to this world, the continuity of the teaching and purification by the Holy Prophet Muhammad, would be intercepted after his appearance, it would be Jesus and not Muhammad, may peace and the blessings of God be upon him, who would purify the Muslims and teach them the Book and the wisdom. But as this is inconceivable in the face of the clear words of the Holy Qur'ān quoted above, Jesus Christ *cannot* appear even as a reformer among the Muslims.

In fact, the finality of prophethood in the person of the Holy Prophet Muhammad, may peace and the blessings of God be upon him, which is one of the basic doctrines of the religion of Islām, is wholly opposed to the appearance or re-appearance of any prophet after him. The Holy Qur'ān teaches us in plain words that prophethood was brought to perfection in the person of the Holy Founder of Islām, and the work attached to the office of a prophet was completed in the revelation granted to him; and therefore as no work remained to be done, no prophet was needed, be he an old prophet or a new one. A prophet could only appear if there was any work for him, but as not the least work which could be done only by a prophet, remains to be done, there is no need of a prophet, and if one comes, there is no place for him in Islām. But it may be said, why then do the most reliable collections of the sayings of the Holy Prophet contain prophecies of the advent of Jesus, son of Mary, if there is no work for a prophet according to the plain teachings of the

---

147. 3:47

Holy Qur'ān? The fact is that prophecies can only be interpreted in such a manner as not to contradict the plain teachings of the Holy Qur'ān, and therefore the prophecy of the advent of Jesus son of Mary must be interpreted in such a manner as to be consistent with the doctrine of the finality of prophethood in the Holy Prophet Muḥammad.

The truth is that the prophecy of the second advent of Jesus Christ could not have meant his personal re-appearance in the world even if it had not been opposed to the fundamental Islāmic doctrine that the Holy Prophet Muḥammad, may peace and the blessings of God be upon him, was the last of the prophets of the world, and this is a point on which the Gospels, which also contain this prophecy, shed the clearest light. A Christian at any rate has not the least reason to expect the personal second coming of Jesus Christ. The Bible tells us that "Elijah went up by a whirlwind into heaven".[148] The matter does not rest there. In another revealed book in the Old Testament collection we are as certainly told of the reappearance of Elijah in the world: "Behold I will send you Elijah the prophet before the coming of the great and dreadful day of the Lord".[149] Thus Elijah, according to the Bible, had not only gone up into heaven, but it was further necessary that he should come back before Christ made his appearance. Such was the faith of the whole of the Israelite nation at the advent of Christ and it was based on the clearest words of their sacred Scriptures.

One of the first questions which confronted the claims of Jesus Christ was, as it should have been: where was Elijah?

> And his disciples asked him, saying, Why then say the scribes that Elias must first come?".[150]

Had the least doubt existed about this prophecy in the mind of Jesus, he would have at once told his disciples that there was no such prophecy, that Elias had died and he would never come back. But no; he admitted that the prophecy was true and that it was necessary that Elias should come.

---

148. 2 Kings 2:11   149. Mal. 4:5   150. Matt. 17:10

And Jesus answered and said unto them, Elias truly shall first come, and restore all things. But I say unto you, that Elias is come already, and they knew him not, but have done unto him whatsoever they listed. Likewise shall also the Son of man suffer of them. Then the disciples understood that he spake unto them of John the Baptist".[151]

How did the disciples come to know that the prophecy of the advent of Elias before the appearance of the Messiah was fulfilled by the coming of John the Baptist? Because of John it had been said: "And he shall go before him in the spirit and power of Elias".[152]

What do all the circumstances narrated above show? It was written that Elias had been received into heaven and there was a prophecy that he would come before the advent of Christ. A question was put to Christ and he said that the prophecy of the coming of Elias had been fulfilled by the appearance of John the Baptist. The reason was that John had come in the spirit and power of Elias. The significance of this is clearly and conclusively this — that when the second advent of a person is spoken of, it is not his personal re-appearance that is meant but the appearance of someone else in his spirit and power. Such is the verdict of Jesus Christ, and it is conclusive against everyone who follows Christ or accepts him as a prophet. No Christian in the world can go against it, and he is bound to put the same interpretation upon the second advent of Jesus Christ as Jesus Christ put upon the second advent of Elias. There is not the slightest difference between the two cases.

If, however, there is no room for a Christian to escape the conclusion arrived at above, a Muslim is equally bound by the judgement of one whom he considers to be a prophet of God. All that the latter can say against that conclusion is that the record is not genuine, but the double testimony of the Old and the New Testaments gives him no ground for such a supposition in this particular case. It cannot be denied that there was a prophecy as to the second advent of Elias; it is equally more certain that Elias

---

151. Matt. 17:11-13   152. Luke 1:17

himself never came back into the world. Moreover, a corruption like this in the Gospels, going as it does against the claims of Jesus, could not have been the work of a Christian, and therefore, it is sure that the question was put to Jesus and he gave this answer. Nor had there been a corruption in the Old Testament in relating this prophecy, for if it had been so, Jesus would not have admitted the truth of the prophecy. The case being so clear against corruption on this particular point, a Muslim is as much bound by the decision of Christ as a Christian, for both admit him to be righteous.

Further consideration shows even more clearly that from a Muslim's point of view, the decision given by Jesus Christ assumes a greater importance. For, whereas there was no objection if Elias himself had re-appeared, there are other grave difficulties besides those referred to above in the personal re-appearance of Jesus Christ. In the first place, the reports which speak of his advent add the words *wa imāmukum minkum*, i.e. and he is your *imām* from among yourselves. These words are conclusive against his being an Israelite. The Messiah that appears among the Muslims must be one of themselves, not an outsider, no prophet but an *imām* or a spiritual guide. Secondly, the most trustworthy collection of reports is the *Sahīh al-Bukhārī* and in this collection we find the two Messiahs, the Israelite prophet Jesus Christ and the Promised Messiah, described differently.

In two reports, the Israelite prophet is described as *ahmar, ja'd*, i.e. *having a white complexion and curly hair*, while in two others narrated in the same chapter the Messiah that is to appear among the Muslims at the time of the great tribulation of the Antichrist is described as *ādam, sabit*, i.e. *of a white colour mixed with black* and *having lank hair* see *Sahīh Bukhārī*, chapter *Bada al-khulq*). Now these two entirely different descriptions settle it conclusively that the Messiah that must appear among the Muslims is a man quite different from the Israelite prophet, and the Holy Prophet Muhammad was not only aware of this fact, but he also made it known to his followers by giving the two descriptions.

In fact, even if it were possible for Jesus Christ to re-appear in the world, he could not have done the great work of regenerating the whole world which the followers of the Holy Prophet Muḥammad, may peace and the blessings of God be upon him, have been doing and can do. So great was the spiritual power of the great World-Prophet that not only did he bring about an immediate transformation of so great a magnitude that the transformations wrought by the reformers of the world dwindle into insignificance before it, but he also imparted that power to his followers in the same high degree so that even prophets have not been able to do what men like Abū Bakr and 'Umar have done. And therefore even to-day, the followers of the Prophet can do what Jesus Christ was not able to do when he was in this world. The Gospels tell us that he could not bring more than five hundred men to the path of rectitude, but to-day we can witness the followers of the Holy Prophet Muḥammad, may peace and the blessings of God be upon him, bringing thousands, nay hundreds of thousands, to the right path. And if Jesus Christ was unable to correct even the small Israelite nation, how could he be a match for the mighty tribulation of the Antichrist? It was a work which could be done only by a follower of the Holy Prophet Muḥammad, and therefore a *Mujaddid*, a reformer promised to the Muslims at the commencement of every century, was entrusted with it. It was the *Mujaddid* of this, the fourteenth century (of Hijrah), who was called a Messiah because he not only appeared in the spirit and the power of the first Messiah, but also corrected the errors connected with the name of a former Messiah, as he himself says:

> As God has given me a light for the Christian people, I have therefore been named the son of Mary.

And he has in fact broken the cross, this being his chief work according to the most authentic reports, because he has shown from the Gospels that the death of Christ did not take place on the cross, as has been wrongly supposed by the Christians for nineteen centuries, but that having escaped with wounds, he died a natural death afterwards, having lived to the ripe old age of 120 years, as a report expressly says. It was "through the blood of his cross"[153] that salvation was purchased:

> And if Christ be not risen, then is our preaching vain, and your faith is also vain.[154]

Christ never died on the cross and he never rose from the dead: the preaching of the Christian missionary is therefore vain and vain is also his faith. The Christian religion laid its foundation on the death of Christ on the cross and his subsequent rising; both these statements have been proved to be utterly wrong on the strength of the historical testimony afforded by the Gospels themselves, and with the foundation the whole superstructure falls to the ground.

THE END

---

153. Col. 1:20   154. I Cor. 15:14

Books on Islam

World-renowned literature produced by
The Ahmadiyya Anjuman Ishā'at Islam, Lahore (Pakistan)

"Probably no man living has done longer or more valuable service for the cause of Islamic revival than Maulana Muhammad Ali of Lahore. His literary works, with those of the late Khwaja Kamal-ud-Din, have given fame and distinction to the Ahmadiyya Movement" — M. Pickthall, famous British Muslim and translator of Holy Quran.

Books by Maulana Muhammad Ali:

The Holy Qur'ān
Pp. lxxvi + 1256

Arabic text, with English translation, exhaustive commentary, comprehensive Introduction, and large Index. Leading English translation. Has since 1917 influenced millions of people all over the world. Model for all later translations. Thoroughly revised in 1951.

"To deny the excellence of Muhammad Ali's translation, the influence it has exercised, and its proselytising utility, would be to deny the light of the sun" — Maulana Abdul Majid Daryabadi, leader of orthodox Muslim opinion in India.

"The first work published by any Muslim with the thoroughness worthy of Quranic scholarship and achieving the standards of modern publications" — Amir Ali in *The Student's Quran*, London, 1961.

The Religion of Islam

Comprehensive and monumental work on the sources, principles, and practices of Islam. First published 1936.

". . . an extremely useful work, almost indispensable to the students of Islam" — Dr Sir Muhammad Iqbal, renowned Muslim philosopher.

"Such a book is greatly needed when in many Muslim countries we see persons eager for the revival of Islam, making mistakes through lack of just this knowledge" — 'Islamic Culture', October 1936.

A Manual of Hadith
Pp. 400

Sayings of Holy Prophet Muhammad on practical life of a Muslim, classified by subject. Arabic text, English translation and explanatory notes.

Muhammad The Prophet

Researched biography of Holy Prophet, sifting authentic details from spurious reports. Corrects many misconceptions regarding Holy Prophet's life.

Early Caliphate
pp. 214

History of Islam under first four Caliphs.

"(1) Muhammad The Prophet, (2) The Early Caliphate, by Muhammad Ali together constitute the most complete and satisfactory history of the early Muslims hitherto compiled in English" — 'Islamic Culture', April 1935.

Living Thoughts of Prophet Muhammad Pp. 150
Life of Holy Prophet, and his teachings on various subjects.

The New World Order Pp. 170
Islam's solution to major modern world problems.

Founder of the Ahmadiyya Movement *1984 U.S.A. edition,* Pp. 100.
Biography of Hazrat Mirza by Maulana Muhammad Ali who worked closely with him for the last eight years of the Founder's life.

Other major publications:

The Teachings of Islam by Hazrat Mirza Ghulam Ahmad. Pp. 226
Brilliant, much-acclaimed exposition of the Islamic path for the physical, moral and spiritual progress of man, first given as a lecture in 1896.
". . . the best and most attractive presentation of the faith of Muhammad which we have yet come across" — 'Theosophical Book Notes'.

Other English translations as well as original Urdu books of Hazrat Mirza are also available.

Muhammad in World Scriptures by Maulana Abdul Haque Vidyarthi. Pp. 1500 in 3 vols.
Unique research by scholar of religious scriptures and languages, showing prophecies about the Holy Prophet Muhammad in all major world scriptures.

Ahmadiyyat in the Service of Islam, by Naseer A. Faruqui, ex-Head of the Pakistan Civil Service. Pp. 149, printed in the U.S.A.
1983 book dealing with the beliefs, claims and achievements of Hazrat Mirza Ghulam Ahmad, and the work of the Lahore Ahmadiyya Movement.

The Great Religions of the World, by Mrs U. Samad. Pp. 258

Anecdotes from the Life of the Prophet Muhammad, by Mumtaz A. Faruqui. Pp. 102

Anecdotes from the Life of the Promised Messiah, by Mumtaz A. Faruqui. Pp. 131

Islam & Christianity by Naseer A. Faruqui

For prices and delivery of these books and inquiries about other books and free literature, please contact: **A.A.I.I.**
    1315 Kingsgate Rd.,
    Columbus, Ohio, 43221 U.S.A.